STO

3-4-60

LORD, TEACH US TO PRAY

F. V. McFatridge

LORD, TEACH US to PRAY

With Jesus in the School of Prayer

BROADMAN PRESS
Nashville, Tennessee

© 1956 · BROADMAN PRESS

Nashville, Tennessee

Second Printing

Library of Congress Card Catalog Number: 56–8674
PRINTED IN THE UNITED STATES OF AMERICA
3.5MY57K.S.P.

To Jewel Grimes McFatridge

Who has graced the preacher's home,
enriched his life, labored by his side,
sustained him by her faith and prayers,
encouraged him by her praise,
and helped him by her loving criticism

And to Our Children,
Mary Bess and Forrest Vernon, Jr.
Who are justifying our faith in them

Preface

Solomon complained a long time ago that, "of making many books there is no end; and much study is a weariness of the flesh" (Eccl. 12:12). But when Job was about to deliver his soul in a great declaration of faith triumphant in adversity, he exclaimed: "Oh that my words were written! Oh that they were inscribed in a book! Oh that with an iron pen . . . they were graven in the rock for ever!" (Job 19:23–24, RSV). I agree with both the jaded and disillusioned king of Israel's golden age and with the suffering patriarch, whose epic poem deals dramatically with so universal a problem that it is as relevant today as it was when it was written. No doubt there are many books that are a "weariness to the flesh," but there are times when the writing of a book becomes an inescapable urge. Walter Russell Bowie, in his recent book *Preaching*, says: "It is not the gift of native eloquence that makes a man significant as he speaks to other men. . . . It is the fact that he has got hold of something—or something has got hold of him—so interesting and important that he can hardly keep still about it."

Prayer is so important in the life of the Christian, and so necessary to any measure of success in the development of a Christian personality, or living successfully as a Christian, or accomplishing anything worth while in Christian service, that not to know the secret of "effectual fervent prayer" is a tragedy. This work is not intended as an exhaustive treatment on prayer in general but is a rather detailed study of the teachings of Jesus to his disciples concerning prayer. When first written, it was given the title: *With Jesus in the School of Prayer,* but the appearance of another book with practically the same title led to the change. The request of the twelve in Luke 11:1 became the new title. It was a fortunate change, for the author has written the revision with the prayer constantly upon his lips, "Lord, teach us to pray!" It is hoped that the reader will have the same prayer in his heart as he reads the following chapters.

No one will ever become a man of prayer by reading books on the subject. When I went up to Burleson College at Greenville, Texas, wearing my first civilian suit since the outbreak of the first world war, Dr. M. T. Tucker, teacher of Bible, said to me: "The only way you'll ever learn to be a preacher is by preaching. We can teach you English and history and Latin and Greek and the Bible, but if the Lord has called you to preach, try to preach somewhere every Sunday. In a schoolhouse or under a tree by the side of the road, wherever you can get a few people to listen to you, preach every opportunity you have." I have never forgotten these words from a humble, consecrated man of God. The only way we ever learn to do anything is by doing it. One does not learn to read by listening to others read, or even by having the teacher read aloud from words written on a blackboard. The child must speak the words himself, as they are pointed out, until he discovers the relation between a group of letters in a particular order, the spoken word, and the object or action the word represents. Nor does one learn arithmetic by seeing problems worked out and having the process explained to him. He must work problems himself. That is universally true and could be illustrated endlessly.

We never really learn anything unless we put it into practice. When I was a boy, I sold books one summer. I approached a farmer who was willing to sit on his plow and talk; but when I told him my business, he said: "No, we don't need any books. We already have one." I said: "But this book is a very valuable book on all the latest methods of farming . . ." and I began my prepared lecture on the merits of the book. He listened a while and then said with a yawn: "Wouldn't do me any good. I wouldn't follow it. *I already know how to do a lot better than I do now.*" I had to admit, in spite of my disappointment, that he had a solid philosophy.

As you and I sit at the feet of the great Teacher in his school of prayer, may we not only hear what he has to say, but may we practice what he teaches until prayer becomes as natural and as necessary as breathing. "Why call ye me, Lord, Lord, and do not the things which I say?" When our hearts are stirred by the contemplation of the wonderful promises of power and victory, and the indescribable blessings that attend the prayer of faith, let us waste no time in proving to ourselves the efficacy of the sort of praying that Jesus taught. If you lay aside the book in the middle of a chapter to pray about a personal problem or need, or to pray for a friend, I shall be amply rewarded for the toil and study that went into the writing. If you read it through and say "Wonderful!" without doing anything about it, *my* reward will be like that of the Pharisee who liked to pray in some public place to be seen of men. And *you* will not be benefited greatly. I have read many books that inspired me and then, have laid them aside as finished. A year or so later I have opened them again, to be reminded of, and rebuked by, the resolutions I had made and failed to put into practice.

Writing these pages in the midst of a busy pastorate
has been a pleasure, and the study required in the preparation of the material has been rewarding indeed to
my own personal prayer life. I am indebted to a great
many sources. Credit has been given wherever possible,
especially where a direct quotation or a particular idea
has been copied. The main source has been the various
translations of the New Testament. Besides the King
James Version, I have used the Revised Standard Version and the translations of Moffatt, Goodspeed, and
Phillips (*Letters to Young Churches* and *The Gospels
in Modern English*), and I am grateful to their copy-
right owners for permission to quote: National Council
of Churches of Christ in America, Harper and Brothers,
University of Chicago Press, and Macmillan Company,
respectively.

The *Expositor's Greek Testament,* G. Campbell
Morgan's *Studies in the Four Gospels,* and the volume
on Matthew by John A. Broadus are among the com-
mentaries consulted. Several books on prayer have been
read, but the notes contain credit to those works that
influenced my treatment.

F. V. McFatridge

Contents

I

The Lost Secret of Power

He was praying at a certain place, and when he stopped one of his disciples said to him, "Lord, teach us to pray, as John taught his disciples."

LUKE 11:1, MOFFATT

The disciples had often listened to Jesus as he prayed; and they were probably shocked at first by the extreme simplicity of his words, the intimate manner in which he talked to God. Wherever he happened to be, he would address his Father as one would speak to a companion who was near at hand, and yet there was no ostentation. Reverence was in his tone, and assurance in his manner. It was as though he knew that the listening ear of God was always attuned, that the Father was always present. The twelve were accustomed to the formal and stately prayers of the rabbis, the incantations of the priests in the Temple, and the loud and eloquent prayers of the Pharisees. Deity was not often addressed as informally as Jesus spoke to the Father.

The disciples also had noticed that Jesus often went apart from them—even from Peter, James, and John —into the desert or upon the mountainside, to spend long periods alone in a communion too sacred to share. At times he spent the whole night in prayer. At other times he arose early in the morning, before the awakening sun had touched the clouds in the eastern sky with rosy fingers, and went apart to pray alone. When he came from these secret sessions of prayer, the disciples noticed that his countenance was marked with a calm assurance, a serene certainty, a joyous sense of power as he faced the problems of the day. *Jesus knew the secret of prayer!*

It was a secret that Israel had lost. Abraham, the friend of God, and Jacob and Joseph and Moses and the long line of ancient prophets had been men of prayer. The Jews of Jesus' day had heard all of their lives about Elijah's contest with the priests of Baal on Mount Carmel. They knew about the time that Elisha was surrounded by the Syrian hosts in the village of Dothan, only to pray that the Lord would open the eyes of the servant that he might see the fiery chariots of the Lord around him. To Jesus' contemporaries, these were events of a remote past. There had been no authentic voice of a prophet heard in Israel for three hundred years. Religion had come to be a burden rather than a lift—the meticulous observance of the letter of the law, of ceremonies and ablutions about which there was constant bickering between the Sadducees and Pharisees. The Promised Land was but a province of Rome, ruled by petty political appointees and patrolled by heathen soldiers. The Temple worship had become the monopoly of a few greedy men who made huge profits from feast days and from animals offered in sacrifice. Prayer, itself, had become a formal thing, designed to impress others with one's piety rather than to reach the ear of God.

The twelve had followed Jesus in the beginning because he spoke "as one having authority," with the certainty of the prophets of old. There was something within them that urged them to leave everything and follow him. They were aware of their own inadequacy, their lack of experience, their ignorance, their lack of faith. The longer they followed Jesus, the keener became their spiritual hunger; they longed with a passion that would brook no denial to know the secret that Jesus knew. He had called them "friends" and had explained things to them that the world was not ready to receive. He had hinted at wonderful things yet to be revealed, at marvelous experiences in store for them.

Perhaps he would tell them the secret, teach them how to pray!

One day, "as he was praying in a certain place, when he ceased"—certainly they would not have intruded while he was praying—they came to him with a very simple yet tremendous request. One of them, perhaps Peter, said: "Lord, teach us to pray!"

The disciples' spokesman did not say, "Lord, teach us *a prayer,*" yet that is what we have made of the Model Prayer. It has become part of a liturgy and nothing more, words to be recited in unison by saint and sinner alike, by believer and unbeliever. These followers of Jesus did not need to know the language of prayer; they could learn that from the Pharisees, if choice words or beautiful sentences or clever phrases were needed. (And we may make a fetish of simplicity, crudeness, and familiarity as well as of eloquence!) What they needed to know was not words or forms in which prayer is framed but what they asked, *"teach us to pray."*

Jesus knew that very soon he and his disciples must undergo a tremendous experience: Gethsemane . . . the betrayal of Judas . . . the mock trials . . . the scourging . . . the jeers of the bloodthirsty mob crying: "Crucify him!". . . the crown of thorns . . . the purple robe of mockery . . . the horror of the cross . . . the dark silence of the tomb. It was an ordeal from which all that was human in him shrank with fear and loathing. He knew that these men who loved him, who knew of his mighty power, would not under-

stand, would not accept, and would be shaken to the
very center of their beings by it all. During the hours
of violence and the three days of burial, anguished
doubts and the very imps of despair would assail them.
They would desperately need to know how to pray.

The need would be no less acute after the resurrection and the wonderful fellowship of the forty days.
The disciples would have a stronger faith, it is true.
There would be a new assurance based upon their
experience of his triumph over death. But they were
to be given a commission, a commission to challenge the
whole world with the life-transforming power of the
gospel of the Son of God. It was a task for which these
humble men—a tax collector, a Zealot, a few fishermen,
and the like—were not within themselves adequate.
They were without money, equipment, political in-
fluences, or social standing. These were the same men
who later would be described by some of their fellow
countrymen as "uneducated, common men" (Acts 4:13,
RSV) or "uncultured persons and mere outsiders"
(Moffatt). They had no adequate organization, no experience, no definite plans. They would soon face the
religious prejudice of a Judaism that had instigated the
crucifixion of their Leader, the jealousy of a government
that called Caesar, "Lord," the intellectual snobbery of
worldly philosophers, the greed and cruelty of men
who worshiped the profits of trade, the materialism that
knows no god but gold and temporal power, the sadism
of pleasure-mad men and women who would crowd the
arena to see a Christian torn by wild beasts or burned at
a stake, demons who cried through human lips, "Let us
alone," and their own weakness that whispered in the
darkness, "What's the use?"

Yes, they would face persecution, threats, imprisonment, ridicule—the laughter of the simple and the sneer of fools—torture, betrayal, poverty, death. They would need to know how to tap unseen resources, how to receive wisdom from above, strength for their weakness, courage for their fears, and patience for their discouragement. They would need to learn the meaning of the promise: "I will not leave you helpless orphans" (John 14:18, Williams). They would need to know how to test the half-remembered promise: "Whatsoever ye ask in my name, that will I do" (John 14:13). *They would need to know how to pray.*

For these reasons, as well as because he loved them, Jesus did teach his disciples how to pray. A large part of the lesson is contained in the true meaning of the Model Prayer. Other teachings are found in the Sermon on the Mount. The teachings of Jesus might be called "A Primer of Prayer," for until the resurrection, the disciples were in the kindergarten of the school of prayer. They finally learned prayer the only way anything is really learned: by practice.

That the disciples really learned how to pray effectively is borne out by the experiences recorded in the book of Acts: they prayed, and power came at Pentecost; they prayed, and three thousand were added to their number in a single day; they prayed, and "the place was shaken where they were assembled"; they prayed and became "of one heart and of one soul"; they prayed and pooled their resources and property to finance the work of witnessing; they prayed, and prison doors were opened; they prayed, and their archenemy, Saul of Tarsus, was converted; they prayed, and the gospel swept across the Roman Empire, until converts

were to be found everywhere, within a single generation. Yes, those early Christians were men and women
of prayer—*they knew the secret of power.*

I am persuaded that not very many of us today know,
and know how to use, the secret the first Christians
knew. All of us who are Christians know *something* of
prayer. Many of us have memories of precious experiences when we knew that we had talked with God. It
may have been in some hour of peril—real or imagined
—to ourselves or a loved one, when we found deliverance and knew that a strong Arm had been made bare
in our defense. It may have been in an hour of deep
sorrow, when we were so numbed by pain and shock
that only the certainty of a divine compassion saved us
from despair. Prayer made a rift in the clouds, let the
sunshine of God's love through, brought the Comforter
to our sides, and brought the realization that "under-
neath are the everlasting arms." It may have been in
some hour when so much depended upon making a decision that we dared not make it alone. We prayed until the right way opened up before us as clearly as
though a pillar of fire were leading.

These are "mountain-top" experiences, too few and
far between. Even such experiences do not teach us les-
sons that abide. After a time, it may seem that our own
wisdom and strength had delivered us. These are isolated examples of what may and should become a familiar pattern of living. Too much of the time, our lives
are lived in the valley of humiliation. Prayer as a certain, always available means of really coming into the
presence of God, talking with him, finding his will, receiving the wisdom, power, and guidance we need constantly, remains an unknown factor in the lives of most
Christians.

Why are there so many inadequate, sin-ridden, frustrated, unhappy, powerless Christians, when the motto of faith is, "I can do all things through Christ which strengtheneth me"? Can it be that we are *afraid* of prayer?

Look what it did for the early Christians!

Who wants to fight wild beasts in the arena?

Who wants to languish in prison, or die upon a stake?

Doesn't being a New Testament Christian cost too much?

Better a live coward than a dead hero!

Or, perhaps, do we want to know the secret of prevailing prayer but want to keep it in reserve, like a spare tire, to be used only in an emergency?

Or can it be that we are too busy watching television, reading the latest "best seller," making money, or "keeping up with the Joneses" that we simply do not have time really to pray?

These studies are for those who really want to know the secret of power.

The first church was a praying church. Since it did not have a building, it probably met from house to house. We have certainly made "progress" today! Why, then, should a critic see church spires as "impotent hands lifted toward heaven in mute confession of their inadequacy to deal with the world's problems"?

Our church buildings stand in the choicest locations. They are dreams of architectural beauty, poems in stone. The bright light of God's sun is filtered through stained glass. Aisles are carpeted in plush; the pews are comfortable and attractive. Indirect lighting throws a soft glow over everything. We have air conditioning; our kitchens are modernly equipped. There are powder

rooms, parlors, committee rooms resembling the directors' rooms of large banks, busy offices, and luxurious
studies.

Look at our teeming Sunday schools: we are reaching
people by the thousands. Our financial reports read like
the balance sheets of big businesses. We have highly-
paid choir directors and young preachers with doctor's
degrees who can promote their programs as effectively as leading business executives. This is not intended to depreciate attractive buildings, hard-working
organizations, or generosity in the financial support of
the Lord's work; but one cannot help but wonder if we
are using rightly and wisely the advantages these
give us.

Why are our many "great" churches seemingly impotent to do very much about vice, poverty, crime, un-
employment, divorce, injustice, oppression, graft, and
political corruption? Why are sin traps for unwary feet
allowed to flourish in the very shadow of such churches?
It is easy enough to say that the church must stay out
of politics and not meddle in business affairs. In fact,
some even dare to quote: "My kingdom is not of this
world." If church members were not concerned with
politics and business, perhaps the indifference of
churches could be justified. But I wonder if we are not
teaching people that one's duty to God and one's duty
to Caesar are separated into airtight compartments in
personality, so that one does not affect the other?

Perhaps we ought to read again what Jesus had to say
about the *status quo* in his day, his scathing denuncia-
tion of some of the things that we have mentioned. Read
his arraignment of religious leaders who would move
heaven and earth to make one proselyte, but who would
not lift a finger to ease humanity's burden. Perhaps we

should listen to John the Baptist—it would seem that when God's only spokesman was "the voice of one crying in the wilderness," a more authentic word was proclaimed than is often heard from today's many pulpits.

Can it be that we have made our "Father's house" everything but a "house of prayer"? If you doubt it, compare the crowd that attends your next fellowship banquet with the crowd you can assemble, quite frankly, for a prayer meeting.

Prayer, rightly understood, will not make our lives an easy dream of unreality, floating on clouds of illusion or riding on hydraulic shock absorbers and foam rubber over the rough places in life. Rightly understood and intelligently and faithfully practiced, prayer will call us back to cross-bearing, to the whole task of the church. It will cause us to put first things first, keep our vision clear to see reality, and give us grace and power for the task committed to us.

If our present church membership, with all the organization and resources that are ours, could achieve one tenth of the zeal and power that New Testament Christianity had—and it can be achieved only when we have learned to pray—we could capture the lost vision, and discover the lost secret of power. With this, the churches of today could, in one year, transform the world in which we live, shake the very foundations of evil, and save all in our civilization that is worth saving.

There are enough books on prayer. Everyone from theologians to movie stars writes books on the power of prayer, the techniques of prayer, testimonies to answered prayer, and so on. Many books seem to be concerned mainly with "getting *things* from God" and are oversimplified. Some regard prayer as a ladder by which we may climb out of the morass of our littleness, our

ineptness, our inadequacies and uncertainties to the
heights of unclouded fellowship. But this approach
tends to make prayer a difficult, mystical thing, suitable
for a hermit who is wholly concerned for his own soul.
Many are fine and valuable; we read them and agree.
Yet prayer remains an unknown quantity for many
Christians.

There are "prayer books," official and unofficial; there
are collections of the prayers of eminent divines. It is
not difficult to learn what men have prayed for or the language that makes prayer beautiful and reverent. But
one feels instinctively that God is less interested in po-
etical language, stately diction, and correct forms than
he is in sincerity of heart, humility of spirit, the depth of
recognized need, and earnestness of purpose.

The world is filled with chaos, with "men's hearts failing them for fear." Hatred, suspicion, and prejudice fill
their minds. The mad race for superbombs, guided missiles, and bombers that travel faster than sound goes on
apace. The best scientific minds are drafted for the task
of inventing new and more efficient means to destroy
men for whom Christ died and to turn cities, homes,
churches, schools, hospitals, and libraries into shapeless
piles of radioactive rubble. Standing above the confusion and chaos, the fear and hatred, the sin and suffering, the bloodshed and violence that turn pleasant
pastoral scenes into an inferno—and yet, somehow,
standing in the midst of all human need—is One who
said: "If ye shall ask anything in my name, I will do
it. . . . Let not your heart be troubled, neither let it
be afraid" (John 14:14, 27).

Do we believe these words?

Why, then, do we labor with feeble minds and impotent hands to create a brave new world, as we en-
ergetically prepare to destroy all that our fathers have

built? Why are our churches not filled with Christians at prayer, asking daily, hourly, *in the name of Jesus,* that faith and sanity and honesty and truth and righteousness and peace shall return to earth?

Why are we, who have been called to be stewards of the grace of God, men of books and eloquence, not men of prayer? Why do we desire to be popular rather than to be prophets?

Have we forgotten, or have we never learned, the power of "the effectual fervent prayer of a righteous man"? Is there no balm in Gilead? Can it be that for multitudes of nominal Christians, in both pew and pulpit, that there is really "no God in Israel"?

What is prayer, anyway? Is it wishful thinking? Is it a man's communion with his own alter ego? Is it a cry into the dark, hoping that somewhere there is a listening Ear, an interested Being, a supernatural Power? Is it some magic formula for getting God on our side, or is it a process that brings us into harmony with the will and purpose of God? Is it an easy method of escaping responsibility for our actions by laying the blame on Deity, or is it a means of finding out the right things to do and finding grace and strength to do the right?

What is the faith that makes prayer effective? Is it blind credulity, rationalized superstition? Is it hope a little stronger than doubt, a forced "will to believe" by which we shout down the clamoring doubts within? Or is it a faculty of the soul that enables us to discern a higher sort of reality than the physical? Is the prayer of faith a sort of "divine legal tender" that we may exchange for miracles at some celestial bank? Or is it a God-given ability that enables us to come into the presence of God and really talk to him?

How shall we pray? Are there certain sacred places in which prayer must be offered in order to be heard?

What physical posture shall we assume? Does it make any real difference? Is there some sort of sacred language to be learned, magic words or phrases that are an open-sesame to God's storehouse of blessings?

For what shall we pray: for escape from the common lot of man—the toils, sorrows, pains, heartaches, disappointments, and denials—or for strength and courage and grace to meet life's reverses like Christian men and women? Shall we pray that God's administration of the universe shall be changed to fit our plans and desires or for an understanding heart that will enable us to fit into God's will and purpose? Shall we pray that what we want shall be ours without effort or for the strength and courage and wisdom to find and follow God's plan for our lives—and having found it, to be content?

These and many other questions task the mind of the earnest seeker after truth; and it may be that no one can answer them all, that some of them may not be answered until we no longer see "in a mirror dimly." There was never but one Authority on prayer: the One who was both God and man, who sat in the councils of God before the world was and yet "became flesh and dwelt among us." God's Son emptied himself of the glory that was his and took the form of a servant. He "was in all points tempted like as we are." He knows both the heart of God and the needs of men. The Old Testament prophets give us their experiences with a prayer-answering God; but Jesus Christ—who is both priest and prophet, the God-man and God in human flesh—became the Way to God for all who receive him. *He knew what prayer really is.* The sole purpose of these studies is that we may join the twelve in the request, "Lord, teach us to pray," and may sit at his feet to learn as they did.

II

The Approach to God in Prayer

Pray then like this:

"Our Father who art in heaven,
Hallowed by thy name."

MATTHEW 6:9, RSV

When you pray, say:

"Father, hallowed be thy name."

LUKE 11:12, RSV

The above quotations from the Revised Standard Version show something of the difference between the wording of the Model Prayer as given by Matthew and by Luke. One explanation is that the prayer was given first in the great Sermon on the Mount, as recorded by Matthew, and upon a later occasion in answer to the request of one of the twelve, as recorded by Luke. It is not my purpose to enter into a detailed discussion of these differences; the interested student may compare the various modern translations for himself. Suffice it to say here that the different wording, the omissions by Luke or the additions by Matthew, seem indubitable proof that our Saviour never intended the Model Prayer to be quoted word for word as a part of a liturgy. Rather, it was meant to teach us how to pray and for what to pray.

For me, as for so many Christians, the form of the prayer that still seems natural is that given in Matthew 6:9–13 in the King James Version. This is what we learned as children, and this is what seems complete.

The concluding doxology—"For thine is the kingdom, and the power, and the glory, for ever. Amen"—seems to belong, even though it is omitted by the earliest manuscripts of the Greek New Testament and hence by the modern English versions. It should be remembered, however, that this omission has been made because the evidence of the Greek New Testament is that the doxology was not part of the prayer as Jesus said it but an addition to Christ's words by later Christians.

How shall we approach God in prayer?

First of all, we must approach him as a Person. Prayer is not a cry into the dark, hoping that somewhere there is Something that will hear and perhaps, be moved to answer. Prayer is the communion of a person with the divine Person. The pantheistic idea that God is not a Person but a sort of benign Influence or Energy—immanent in all nature, working creatively through natural laws—is fundamentally anti-Christian. To define God as a splendid Idea or Ideal, the sum total of all good, seems to me to rob us both of God and of the dignity of the individual. Without a personal God, man would be the helpless victim of a mechanistic universe. His greatest tragedy would be the ability to think and dream, for he imagines he was made in the image of God and thinks that he is free and dreams of immortality. Man would be far better off in a universe without a personal God if he were incapable of thinking and feeling. The childish concept of God as "a great big Man with a beard" needs revision as we grow; *but the child who thinks thus is infinitely nearer the truth, if Jesus knew and spoke truth, than the erudite scholar who seeks to define God as less than personal.* God is spirit, yes; but he is a Person whom we may call "Father."

Since man was created in the (spiritual) image of

God, and that which changed man from a lump of inanimate clay into a "living soul" was God himself; all the attributes of the spiritual self that we call personality come from God. God possesses, in infinite perfection, all the qualities that make us persons. We have intelligence; he has all wisdom. We have emotions; love, mercy, and compassion belong to God. We have wills, by which we determine our actions and attitudes; the will of God is supreme. We are conscious of moral compulsion, a categorical imperative whose violation causes us inward pain and a sense of guilt; in God, righteousness is complete and perfect. "Shew us the Father, and it sufficeth us," begged Philip, expressing the deep hunger of the human soul from the dawn of time; and Jesus answered, "He that hath seen me hath seen the Father" (14:8–9). Jesus was a man; he was also God.

How can one pray at all, if not to a Person? Can a man talk to Natural Law, to the law of gravity, say? Can he express the thoughts that trouble him to Energy: to electricity, vibrations, or the power that resides in the atom? Can he ask an Idea, or even the Great Unknown First Cause, for comfort, wisdom, and guidance? Can a man ask *It* to forgive sins? Jeremiah ridiculed idolatrous Israel for saying "to a tree, 'You are my Father,' and to a stone 'You gave me birth' " (Jer. 2:27, RSV). I once saw a drunk man talking to the blackened stump of a tree, asking it alternately for a drink and for assistance in getting home. Is our praying like that? Are we intoxicated with superstitious ideas when we pray, talking to ourselves or to a fantasy of the mind or to an impersonal Force, under the mistaken idea that we are talking to a Person? Surely such a concept of God is no better than an idol of wood or stone such as the heathen worship. Their "faith" ascribes personality to their idols. Even

though this may be a grotesque and perverted personality, the idol represents a Being rather than a Force.

Second, we are to approach God in prayer with confidence, a simple, childlike trust. The Old Testament
often pictured God as awe-inspiring and terrible. He
was Lawgiver, Judge, and Supreme Ruler. Only the
high priest went into the holy of holies; and even that
was only once a year, on the Day of Atonement. Individuals such as Abraham and Moses whose courageous
faith enabled them to come into God's presence were
recognized as exceptional. The prophets thundered
forth God's judgment upon sin and sinners, although
their message was always mixed with God's plea for the
disobedient to return to him and receive his mercy and
forgiveness. The writer of Hebrews has pictured in un-
forgettable language the difference between the Old
Testament and the New:

For ye are not come unto the mount that might be
touched, and that burned with fire, nor unto blackness, and
darkness, and tempest, and the sound of a trumpet, and the
voice of words; which voice they that heard intreated that
the word should not be spoken to them any more. . . . But
ye are come unto mount Sion, and unto the city of the living
God, the heavenly Jerusalem, and to an innumerable company of angels, to the general assembly and church of the
firstborn, which are written in heaven, and to God the
Judge of all, and to the spirits of just men made perfect, and
to Jesus the mediator of the new covenant (Heb. 12:18–19,
22–24).

Jesus, the Way to God, taught us to address God as
"our Father" and to come to him as simply and confi-
dently as my children used to rush into my study when
I was in the midst of sermon preparation, to bring their
childish needs and desires or "just to be with Daddy."

(I never held to the idea that I must be inaccessible and unapproachable when preparing sermons, for sermons must relate themselves to life if they are to do any good.)

"For whoever would draw near to God must believe that He exists and that he rewards those who seek him" (Heb. 11:6, RSV). With confident faith that God loves us and hears us, we are to come into his presence boldly, knowing that he is never too busy with the affairs of this vast universe to be concerned about our needs.

But we are also to approach God with reverence. "Hallowed be thy name." To the modern mind and temperament, there may seem to be a paradox in addressing God as Father and then expressing reverence for his name. There are two extreme views of the parent-child relationship. One extreme holds that the father is a tyrant, austere, unapproachable, exacting, demanding unquestioning obedience and acceptance of his views and judgments. The other extreme regards the father as merely the breadwinner, whose only function is to provide money for the family to spend. Apart from this, he should stay in the background as much as possible. He is thought of as "the old man" whose ideas on most things are funny and out of date. The breakdown in parental authority and home discipline is probably due to two factors: the modern idea that children must be allowed to "express their personalities" in their own way and the unconcern of fathers who are too busy making money or living their own lives to take an active interest in their children's moral and spiritual welfare. If father is little more than a source of handouts, it is probably his own fault; for the little child reveres his father, trusts him, and depends upon him.

In thinking of God as our Father, we need to keep the

biblical concept of fatherhood in mind. God's will is supreme, and his laws are unchangeable and obligatory. His authority is unquestioned, but his laws are never arbitrary, nor are his commands selfish or the result of whim or caprice. They are designed for our own good, out of his wisdom. Jesus said, "The sabbath was made for man, and not man for the sabbath" (Mark 2:27), but he did not mean that men should ignore the sabbath.

There is nothing incompatible between regarding God with the confidence and trust and love suggested by the term "Father" and yet giving him due reverence. Adopting a tone of familiarity in addressing God in public prayer, addressing him as "you" instead of as "thou," has always seemed to me to smack of irreverence, to reduce God to our level. "My thoughts are not your thoughts, neither are your ways my ways, saith the Lord. For as the heavens are higher than the earth, so are my ways higher than your ways, and my thoughts than your thoughts" (Isa. 55:8–9). The Third Commandment seeks to prevent making the name of God commonplace: "Thou shalt not take the name of the Lord thy God in vain" (Exod. 20:7). The devout Jews had such reverence for the ineffable name that it was not ordinarily pronounced. Most people think that the profane use of God's name is the only violation of this commandment. Although such use is a major sin of irreverence that shows disrespect for God, one's self, and those who hear, the profane person is not the only one who is guilty of the sin of irreverence. Profanity in speech may be the result of ignorance, but irreverence takes many forms.

Dr. Joseph R. Sizoo has one chapter in a recent book on "The Lost Sense of Wonder," in which he says: "We belong to a generation which is suffering from one thing above all other things: it is the lost sense of wonder. We no longer believe that the impossible can happen. . . . We have lost sight of the God who makes grass to grow upon the mountains. . . . If somehow we could have a fresh baptism or rebirth of faith in the God of the incredible, we would meet the future with greater serenity and courage." [1] It does seem strange that in an age when mere men have learned to perform "miracles" through an expanding knowledge of the universe, there should be doubt about the power of the God who made the universe. But there is. Our achievements have made us proud instead of increasing our wonder and awe for the Creator who has put so many things within our reach, mysterious powers so vast that we have as yet only touched the borders of knowledge. Instead of saying, "Speak, Lord; for thy servant heareth," we are apt to say, "Listen, God; man is talking."

Who may truly call God, "Father"?

The universal fatherhood of God and the brotherhood of all men without regeneration are beautiful ideas, but they are not true. All men are *potentially* the children of God through faith in Jesus Christ: Jew and Gentile, slave and free, wise and foolish, educated and ignorant. This is true of all nationalities: German, French, Russian, Italian, English, Chinese, Japanese, African. It applies to all races: white, yellow, black, brown, red. "As many as received him [the divine Logos], to them gave he power [*exousia*, "right," "privilege," "authority"] *to become* the sons of God, even to them that believe on his name: which were born, not of blood, nor of the will of the flesh, nor of the will of man, but of God" (John 1:12-13). The driving power of all missionary endeavor

---

[1] Joseph R. Sizoo, *Preaching Unashamed* (New York: Abingdon-Cokesbury Press, 1949), pp. 90-91.

is that Christ commanded us to preach his gospel to all men in order that they might hear, believe, and *become* the children of God. Since Adam's transgression, no man is by nature the child of God. He becomes such only by God's redeeming grace. The Jewish people of Jesus' time said, "We have one father, even God." To this, the Lord replied, "If God were your Father, ye would love me. . . . Ye are of your father the devil, and the lusts of your father ye will do" (John 8:41–44). This is to the children of the Covenant! No one becomes a child of God without saving faith. Faith is prerequisite to effective prayer, and faith begins with trusting Christ as Saviour.

An experience in France during World War I is still vivid in my memory. America's civilian army was new, and the need for chaplains was not as clearly recognized as in the recent war. I had not attended a religious service for a year and knew when Sunday came only because I did not have to drill. On a particular Sunday, I went with a group of boys on a sight-seeing tour that included several visits to wine shops and much horseplay. When I lay down on my bunk that night, I felt very depressed. I suddenly remembered that this was the Lord's Day, and a sense of shame and guilt assailed me.

Early in childhood I had formed the habit of "saying my prayers" before going to sleep. I began, "Our Father," and stopped in consternation. *Was God my Father?* Then memory took me back to the little country church I had attended as a boy, back to the hour when God became my Father indeed and I became his child! I could see the old country preacher, and hear his voice as he proclaimed the redeeming grace of God through Jesus Christ. I remembered how I felt as, for the first time, I realized he was talking to me. I remembered the simple plea with which he closed: "Is he precious to you? Do you love him? Will you trust him now as your Saviour?" Something seemed to lift me out of my seat, and I found myself standing before God's messenger, with tears streaming down my face, as all my being responded to the preacher's plea. I did love him; I did trust him. I gave myself to him as completely as I knew how. Neighbors, kinfolk, and friends gathered around me, welcoming me into the fold of the redeemed. As I walked home down country lanes, I walked in a new world, my Father's world.

Lying on an army cot in France with the fumes of cheap wine around my head, I relived that experience. Such a transport of joy filled my heart that I forgot the rest of the Lord's Prayer. I poured out a confession of sin and wandering, and sought forgiveness. My prayer was not that of a culprit before a stern judge but of a wayward son to his Father who loved him, for God had become my Father when I had accepted Christ.

The idea of the universal fatherhood of God implies that men who reject or ignore Jesus Christ may call God, "Father." Logically, it minimizes the importance of regeneration and makes Christ's atonement unnecessary. God hears sinners. Sometimes, no doubt, their prayers are answered; but the secret of prayer is for the children of God.

III

The Approach to God in Prayer

(Continued)

Thy kingdom come,
Thy will be done,
    On earth as it is in heaven.
                    MATTHEW 6:10, RSV

Thy kingdom come.
                    LUKE 11:2, RSV

In the preceding chapter we have seen that Jesus taught his disciples to come to God as children to their Father, in an attitude of confidence, trust, love, and reverence. Here he goes a step further: in coming to God in prayer we acknowledge him as Sovereign, whose will is supreme and must be done. In the beginning of effective prayer the worshiper also must rightly relate himself to the kingdom of God.

Years ago I heard Dr. S. J. Porter speak to a large gathering at Woodlake Baptist Encampment near Sherman, Texas, on the Lord's Prayer. He analyzed the approach to God in the Model Prayer under such headings as: children addressing their Heavenly Father, worshipers adoring their God, subjects acknowledging their King, and servants pledging obedience. I do not know whether that address has ever been published, but I desire to give credit to the man who opened my eyes to the riches of this prayer thirty years ago.

"Oh thou that hearest prayer, unto thee shall all flesh come" (Psalm 66:2), sang the psalmist, and no doubt all men who have heard of the God who hears and answers prayer have at some time prayed to him, even if they erected their altar, "To an unknown God." During the recent world war, a sentence became famous: "There are no atheists in foxholes." It was not, as some optimistic people believed, evidence that the horrors and dangers of war made men Christians. Having served as a private in an artillery regiment that went to France during World War I, I can bear testimony that there were impromptu prayer meetings held on shipboard—when an unidentified submarine menaced the convoy—by men whose ordinary use of the name of God was in profanity. When the scare was over, the prayer meetings turned into "crap" games.

In times of sudden stress or great peril, men pray. It may be that their prayer is no more than a cry into the dark for help from unknown powers. Macauley has reminded us that the most ignorant, primitive, or savage people—without written language, government, or towns—have shrines, altars, sacred places, and prayers. What right have we to forbid anyone to pray or to say dogmatically that God never hears nor heeds the prayers of sinners? Who but God is able to judge whether a man is sincere or has faith, even when he seems to us as unworthy as the publican seemed to the Pharisee?

But this book is a study of prayer as the secret of power given to the children of God, prayer as a means of actual communion with God, prayer that will lift a man out of weakness, futility, sin, uncertainty, and failure to strength, efficiency, righteousness, assurance, and triumph. It is a study of prayer as a means of becoming, first of all, the men and women God wants us to be. It is concerned with our receiving the power and wisdom and guidance that God would give us. Before the prodigal son "came to himself" and saw himself as he was, stripped of all his illusions, his prayer was, "Give me . . ." But after the experience in the hog pen that started him on the painful journey back to his father's house, his prayer became, "Make me . . ." (Luke 15:11–19). We are going to see that the promises made concerning prayer, while unlimited, are not unconditional. The promises are for believers, children of God through faith in Jesus Christ, who are rightly related to God so that they can ask "in the name of Jesus."

Achieving the attitudes taught in the Model Prayer is itself the answer to the most important prayer a man can pray. To know that we are the children of God, that we have put "the kingdom of God and his righteousness" first and are gladly and gloriously submissive to the perfect will of God does indeed—to quote the words used every Sunday morning by a deacon in my first pastorate—put us "on praying ground and pleading terms." Another deacon, in a church where I was preaching the series of sermons out of which this book grew, said to me, "I see you are right, of course. But you make me doubt that I have ever really prayed the Lord's Prayer."

I answered, "But wouldn't you like to?"

With deep emotion he replied: "I certainly would . . . and I intend, with the help of God, to be able to do so."

Jesus never made discipleship an easy matter. Remember the rich young ruler. Remember when "many of his disciples went back, and walked no more with him." He turned to the twelve and said, "Will ye also go away?" (John 6:66–67). He did not alter the requirements of discipleship. And we have no right or authority to alter his terms.

This verse may be regarded as a transition from approach to petition, for it contains elements of both. One cannot truly pray, "Thy kingdom come. Thy will be done," who does not acknowledge Christ as King, and who is not ready and anxious to do God's will himself. Praying for the advancement of Christ's kingdom—until men everywhere shall do his will *before* asking for daily bread, the forgiveness of sins, or guidance and deliverance—is the highest form of petition. This is putting the kingdom of God and his righteousness first.

The most tragic fault of an overeager "evangelism" that is mainly concerned with "visible results" is that people get the impression that they can "accept" Christ as Saviour without yielding to him as the Lord and Master of their lives. Such "evangelism," I am persuaded, gets people's names on church books but not on the Lamb's book of life; it builds up the "evangelist's" reputation but not the body of Christ; it advances "religion" but not the kingdom of God. Christ is not divided. He is both Saviour and Lord. We cannot accept his saviourhood without acknowledging his lordship. It may be that the evangelist is sincere, but mistaken sincerity is no substitute for truth. The evangelist may proceed on the theory: "Get them into the church, and then lead them to a deeper committal." But this is not the way it usually works. Many who respond to such an invitation think they are saved "once and for all," and others, realizing that they are not really changed, privately regard the whole thing as an illusion. People in the first group increase the number of "nominal Christians" in our churches, while those in the second drift away and are more difficult to bring to Christ than ever.

Paul wrote, "I know whom I have believed, and am persuaded that he is able to keep *that which I have committed* unto him against that day" (2 Tim. 1:12). What had Paul committed unto Christ? He had given himself and his all, so that he could write without hypocrisy, "Christ liveth in me" (Gal. 2:20), and, "For me to live is Christ" (Phil. 1:21). He signed himself "a servant of Jesus Christ," and the word translated "servant" actually means "slave." Only after we have made the committal that Paul made can we speak with Paul's assurance. I once heard a preacher who was addicted to unusual expressions talk about people who said to him, "I won't be at church Sunday, but I'll be with you in spirit." He said: "If you are not coming, don't send your spirit around. I can't get anywhere preaching to disembodied spirits; it's a spooky business anyway." Do not say to God, "I'll give you my soul, but my life is my own, to live as I think best."

When Jesus taught us to pray, "Thy kingdom come," exactly what did he mean? It is easy to answer that he was merely using a phrase that was common in prayer in his day. "Even the Rabbis said, that is no prayer in which no mention of the kingdom is made." [1] We know that the idea of the rabbis concerning the kingdom was very different from that of Jesus. Their conception was that the earthly kingdom of Israel, with a monarch on David's throne, was synonymous with the kingdom of God—much as Roman Catholics believe that their organization, with the hierarchy and the pope at its head, is synonymous with the church, the body of Christ.

Probably all evangelical Christians can agree that the kingdom of God and the kingdom of Christ are the same. I believe that we can agree that Christ's kingdom is a spiritual kingdom, "not of this world," and that it

---

[1] Alexander Balmain Bruce, "The Synoptic Gospels," in *The Expositor's Greek Testament* (Grand Rapids, Mich.: Wm. B. Eerdmans Publishing Company, n.d.), I, 120.

involves the reign of God in the hearts and lives of men who accept it.

But what do we mean by: "Thy kingdom come"? Here, unfortunately, we are divided, and not along denominational lines. To some, this means a literal fulfilment of Revelation 20, although I doubt that many believe the chain with which Satan is bound is a literal chain of iron or steel. These Christians think of the coming of the kingdom as a future event, preceded by the battle of Armageddon and involving a reign on earth of a thousand years, with Satan bound. In this view, there must be a final war, in which Satan is able to gather forces *after* the millennial reign that number as the sand of the sea. I once heard a speaker at a denominational gathering, in a section where the notes to the Scofield Bible were virtually regarded as part of the inerrant Word of God, refer to Christ as "prophet, priest, and king" and hasten to correct himself by saying, "Christ is not king now, but he is going to be." Jesus said when he gave the Great Commission: "All authority in heaven and on earth *has been given* to me" (Matt. 28:18, RSV).

I could not resist saying, "Christ is my King now and has been since I believed." I did not mean that I had always been an obedient subject, but I knew that I had been "delivered . . . from the power of darkness, and . . . translated . . . into the kingdom of his dear son" (Col. 1:13). Without entering further into this question, one observation seems justified. Regarding the coming of the kingdom as something to be argued about but not acted upon is an easy escape from responsibility. It furnishes the same escape from responsibility toward Christ's kingdom that hyper-Calvinism did from the missionary challenge. This latter attitude was well summed up in a remark attributed to J. C. Ryland, an English Baptist preacher, who, upon hearing William Carey make an impassioned plea for obedience to the Great Commission, was reported to have said, "Young man, sit down, sit down. . . . When God pleases to convert the heathen, He'll do it without consulting you or me." [2]

The ultradispensational view of the kingdom offers an easy escape from the necessity of trying to get Christians to apply the principles of Christ to all areas of living, including such difficult ones as racial relationships, economics, politics, private and public morality, and family relationships. In short, this view does not take God's purpose seriously: "that you may be blameless and innocent, children of God without blemish in the midst of a crooked and perverse generation, among whom you shine as lights in the world" (Phil. 2:15, RSV). The gospel does indeed deal with men as individuals but as individuals who are members of society, who vote, engage in business, and enter politics. In all of life's areas, Christians are called to labor to make the kingdom of God a reality.

Christ's kingdom is advancing, although sometimes it seems that we are thrown back into the Dark Ages. It requires a strong faith to sing:

> The kingdom *is* coming, O tell ye the story,
>> God's banner exalted shall be!
> The earth shall be full of His knowledge and glory,
>> As waters that cover the sea!
>
> MARY B. C. SLADE

Its coming in completeness is yet future. "The kingdoms of this world are become the kingdoms of our

---

[2] See S. Pearce Carey, *William Carey* (3d ed.; New York: George H. Doran, 1924), p. 50.

Lord, and of his Christ; and he shall reign for ever and ever" (Rev. 11:15). As Moffatt puts it, "The rule of the world has passed to our Lord and his Christ, and he shall reign for ever and ever." That we may grasp what it means, let us add to the word pictures of the prophets, these lines from the pen of Henry Warburton Hawkes:

Thy Kingdom come! then all the din of war
    Like some dark dream shall vanish with the night!
Peace, holy peace, her myriad gifts shall pour,
    Resting secure from danger and affright.

Thy kingdom come! no more shall deeds of shame
    Brutish and base, destroy the soul divine;
Bright with Thy love's all-purifying flame
    Thy human temples evermore shall shine.

Thy kingdom come! mad greed for wealth and power
    No more shall grind the weaklings in the dust;
Then mind and strength shall share Thy ample dower,
    Brothers in Thee, and one in sacred trust.[3]

Make this petition part of every prayer. Let us work as well as pray, remembering always that we are God's children and citizens of his kingdom, and that we are to work as well as watch and pray. We are not to pray, "Thy kingdom come. Thy will be done," and then dismiss this from our consideration or concern.

The interests of Christ's kingdom should be related to all that we pray for. For ourselves, we should ask the things that will make us better citizens of Christ's kingdom, more efficient workers in his vineyard. Furthermore, our requests are to be tempered by desiring only

---

[3] From " 'Thy Kingdom Come!' O Lord" in *Masterpieces of Religious Verse,* ed. James Dalton Morrison (New York: Harper and Brothers, 1948), pp. 447–448; used by permission.

those things that are in accord with God's will for us. If that will does not agree with our desires, we should remember that we are children who are sure of a Father's love and citizens who have a benevolent Sovereign. Paul prayed earnestly that the "thorn in the flesh," the "messenger of Satan," might be removed. But the answer was: "My grace is sufficient for thee: for my strength is made perfect in weakness" (2 Cor. 12:7–10). When Paul wrote about it, he was convinced that the "thorn in the flesh" (whatever it was) was to prevent him from being "exalted above measure." Praying in submission to God's will is not a limitation on prayer. Quite the contrary, for his will is always best—*best for us*.

IV

The Prayer for Daily Bread

Give us day by day our daily bread.

Luke 11:3

It may strike the idealist as a strange descent from so majestic a petition as, "Thy Kingdom come. Thy will be done in earth, as it is in heaven," to a prosaic plea for enough food for the day's need. From thoughts that compass the universe of time and eternity, as we identify ourselves with the onward sweep of that spiritual kingdom that shall conquer and subdue all its foes, we turn to thoughts of supplying our stomachs. The person who has always lived in the midst of plenty, whose only concern for food has been, "What shall we have for dinner today?" or, "Shall we dine out or eat at home?" may think of food as unimportant or prosaic. He should remember that there are times and conditions when enough food to sustain life becomes the supreme concern.

Since this is the only petition in the Model Prayer that concerns material things, it is worthy of careful consideration. We will notice that it is not a prayer for wealth or luxury, not for full barns with "food for many years," not for a bank account, stocks and bonds, houses and lands, a fine car, or any of the things that men depend upon for security or to satisfy and flatter their egos. It is simply a prayer that there shall be a supply, day by day, for that day's needs.

In the first place, this prayer recognizes God as the owner and giver of all things. The careless and impious unbeliever is apt to feel that he has the right to take

31

anything that is not fenced in, nailed down, or well defended, since everything belongs to the man who is smart enough and strong enough to take it. But the Christian realizes that "the earth is the Lord's, and the fulness thereof; the world, and they that dwell therein" (Psalm 24:1). "The silver is mine, and the gold is mine, saith the Lord of hosts" (Hag. 2:8). "Every beast of the forest is mine, and the cattle upon a thousand hills" (Psalm 50:10). God is also the Giver. "Every good gift and every perfect gift is from above, and cometh down from the Father of lights, with whom there is no variableness, neither shadow of turning" (James 1:17), wrote the man who was a half brother of Jesus in the flesh and a brother in the faith. The Old Testament reminds us that "it is he that giveth thee power to get wealth" (Deut. 8:18).

Since God is the owner and giver and we are children dependent upon his bounty, asking for our material needs day by day is a very vital part of prayer. Whether or not we are now in immediate need, whether our barns are full or empty, whether our pocketbooks are lean or fat, asking God to supply our daily needs is good spiritual psychology. It keeps us humbly aware of our true source of supply. It is also good common sense. Barns burn down. Banks fail. Thieves break in and steal. Land washes away or loses its fertility. Sickness or misfortune dissipates carefully hoarded supplies. Only God remains "the same yesterday, and to day, and for ever" (Heb. 13:8). He alone never loses his power, relaxes his vigilance, or ceases his care for us.

To pray for daily bread does not mean, of course, that we are to sit down in idleness and expect God to feed us as he fed Elijah by the ravens. The way he fed the children of Israel with literal "bread from heaven" is not his usual way. Nor does this mean that we are to waste what God provides today, refusing to store up for winter out of the abundance of summer and fall. Nor does it justify the improvidence of failing to provide in youth for the needs of old age. It does not justify destroying the fertility of the soil or exploiting the natural resources that should be preserved for posterity. This petition means, rather, that we are to use the talents, wisdom, and ability God has given us to provide for our own needs, trusting him to help us and give success to our efforts. God put the fertility in the soil, the germ of life into the seed. The seasons are his and the powers of nature: the sunshine and rain to nourish the growing plants, the wind that carries the pollen from tassel to stamen, even the bees that fertilize the blossoms. He expects us to cultivate the soil and gather the harvest.

This prayer teaches us also that God is concerned with, and interested in, our physical and material needs. It is a mistaken idea that the physical and material are essentially evil and that the spiritual is necessarily good. When God had finished creating the physical universe, he saw that it was "very good." On the other hand, Paul warned us of "spiritual wickedness in high places" (Eph. 6:12). It is wrong to divide life into the sacred and the secular. For the Christian, all things are sacred; for the unbeliever, nothing is sacred. It is not wealth but the inordinate love of wealth for wealth's sake that is "the root of all evil" (1 Tim. 6:10). Money builds churches or brothels, hospitals or battleships. It enables missionaries to go out preaching or armies to go out killing. Money may be used to feed the hungry, clothe the naked, and minister to the sick and helpless, or to crush and oppress the weak. It will buy either Bibles or bullets. Nothing that God created is evil; evil comes with the wrong use of that which within itself is "very good."

The feeding of Israel in the wilderness is a splendid object lesson of day-by-day dependence on God. The manna fell in abundance each night, covering the ground like "hoar frost." Each family was to gather *enough for that day's need,* except that upon the sixth day a double portion was gathered to last over the sabbath. Some were greedy (and unbelieving) and gathered more than was needed. The surplus turned sour and became filled with worms. God fed Israel thus for forty years, but when the people reached the Promised Land, where they could secure food for themselves, the manna ceased. *It was God's method, not his providential care, that changed.* The widow who fed God's prophet during a famine, without diminishing the flour in the barrel or the oil in the cruse, is an example of God's method in an emergency. Jesus' feeding the five thousand on the five loaves and two fishes is another. When Jesus saw a multitude following him *merely* for the loaves and fishes, he sent them away, simply by stating the terms of discipleship.

During my student days at Southwestern Baptist Theological Seminary, I lived, like many another, almost completely on faith. There were times that I could have been arrested according to a strict interpretation of the law for "having no visible means of support." The larder often was all but empty, and the pocketbook *was* empty. There were times when the rent was due, and there was no money with which to pay it. There were unexpected doctors' bills. A practically new "T model" had to be put on blocks and have the air let out of the tires because there was no money for a license tag or gasoline. Students with wives and little children learned to pray for daily bread. The answer always came to those whose consciousness of the divine call and faith in God was able to stand the test. Some of the answers seemed like miracles. I always knew the secondary sources of the help that came—a sixteen-hour job on Saturday working in a salvage grocery sale, with pay in enough groceries for a week; an odd job painting a house in off hours, or assisting another student who was a paper hanger; a chance to supply the pulpit of some country church. But I knew that God was the Giver—in answer to prayer.

At one time I resigned a pastorate with no other in view. The time was fast approaching when the date I had set to finish my work would arrive. I felt it obligatory that I move out of the parsonage when the time came. One night I prayed until past midnight, not saying much in words but waiting on the Lord. I was able then to leave the matter in his hands and go soundly asleep. The next morning's mail brought an invitation from a church whose location I had to look up on the map. I went, and it was the beginning of five and a half years of fruitful and joyous service. But, someone might object, the letter was already on its way before I prayed that night. Had it not been for that desperate season of importunate prayer, I never would have gone into that pulpit with the certainty that the invitation was of God. God often anticipates our needs, just as faith is to anticipate the answer. "And all things, whatsoever ye shall ask in prayer, believing, ye shall receive" (Matt. 21:22).

What is included in "daily bread"? Life in today's world is infinitely more complex than in more primitive times. We have many more needs, and we are increasingly dependent on many others. In one rural parsonage where we lived, everything except the heat depended upon electricity. The water supply was from a deep well with an electric pump, and the kitchen range was electric. One Christmas, just after the noon meal, a main fuse burned out, and there was no spare. All the stores were closed in the nearby city, and there was a houseful of guests for supper and the night. What a mess! Our well-being depends on so many little things. It is not just bread that we need, but money to pay the gas bill, the electric bill, the water bill, to buy gas and oil and tires for the car that is essential to our work, and so on. We can no longer shoulder an axe and go into the woods for fuel, or carry water from the spring.

The prayer for daily bread includes prayer about what profession we shall choose or what vocation we shall follow, about securing and keeping work, about the use of time, money, and life itself. It is, in short, asking God to be our senior Partner. This was the attitude on which the late J. L. Kraft built his cheese business. Mr. Kraft used to tell of the time he stopped his old gray horse in the shade of a tree to ask God to take charge of his business and share in its profits.

How different is the attitude of some people who want to receive without making any corresponding commitment! During the depression I was one of a committee of pastors asked to supervise the distribution of flour and other commodities to the needy. In one large family, we found such amazing destitution that we stretched our own meager funds to supply food for hungry mouths. Used clothing was found to cover nakedness. On Saturday night, this whole family was lined up at the ticket window of a movie theater, paying fifteen or twenty-five cents each for admission. The stalwart head of another family to which the Methodist pastor and I had carried food at our expense was in town the next day, quite drunk. Here were people who could find money for movies or "bootleg" whiskey while preachers scrambled to provide them with food. The prayer for daily bread should proceed from those who acknowledge God as Sovereign. It should be in line with the will of God.

To pray in simplicity and with implicit trust for the day-to-day supply for one's physical needs delivers us from the haunting fear of insecurity. G. Ernest Thomas, in his book *Faith Can Master Fear,* lists the fear of insecurity as one of the major fears that few escape. It is one of the major drives of the human personality. After pointing out that the advances men have made in the control of the elements and the exploitation of natural resources ought to make our generation feel more secure than any of the past, he quotes from a poem by James Norman Hall:

> The thing that numbs the heart is this:
>   That men cannot devise
> Some scheme of life to banish fear
>   That lurks in most men's eyes.
>
> Fear of the lack of shelter, food,
>   And fires for winter's cold;
> Fear of his children's lacking these,
>   This in a world so old.[1]

Relief workers who ministered to the thousands of orphaned and starving children in Europe and Asia following the holocaust of World War II found that even after they had made the children accustomed to good, regular meals, many could not sleep for fear that tomorrow they would be hungry again. Someone hit upon the idea of giving each child a piece of bread to hold. The children fell asleep immediately with smiles on their

---

[1] G. Ernest Thomas, *Faith Can Master Fear* (New York: Fleming H. Revell Company, 1950), p. 58.

faces, secure in the certainty that there was food for
tomorrow. Of course, their security depended infinitely
more upon the love, generosity, and ability of the relief
workers than upon the bread within their grasp, but the
memory of their past suffering and of the inhumanity of
other adults was too strong for such reasoning.

Thus we, who think that our security depends upon
things, become obsessed with the idea of securing property and money so that there will never be a time when
we or ours shall lack the necessary funds to purchase
what we need or want. This is a hopeless delusion.
There was a time in Germany when a bushel basket of
impressive-looking currency was required to buy a loaf
of bread. I have talked to some Latvian refugees who
were brought to this country penniless. Among them
were men who had owned fertile farms with brick
houses and herds of livestock. There were ex-bankers,
doctors, lawyers, ex-merchants, and a woman with a
Ph.D. degree who was working as a scrub woman. One
could thrill with pride in the human spirit that enabled
these people to work to establish themselves anew. At
the same time, their losses created a deep sympathy, for
their plight illustrates the deceitfulness of riches. The
rich man worries more than the poor man; he has more
to worry about!

Trust in a paternalistic government that seeks to
guarantee every man "freedom from want," regardless
of his worth, is even greater folly. Government has
nothing that it does not take from its citizens in one
form of taxes or another. It can only take from the rich
and give to the poor, take from the provident and give
to the improvident, take from the workers and give to
the shirkers. Such government tends to destroy incentive to toil and save, thus leading to slave labor as its

ultimate alternative. Those who have been deluded by the dream of paternalism also forget that a large share of that which the government takes must be used to pay the collectors and distributors; a larger share is wasted. Only a trickle finally comes to provide the masses "freedom from want."

In the great Sermon on the Mount, Jesus has shown instead the true way to escape the fear of insecurity. Regarded by some as an impractical dream, we shall one day discover his way to be the only realism:

> Do not worry about life, wondering what you will have to eat or drink, or about your body, wondering what you will have to wear. Is not life more important than food, and the body than clothes? . . . So do not worry and say, "What shall we have to eat?" or "What shall we have to drink?" . . . For these are all things the heathen are in pursuit of, and your heavenly Father knows well that you need all this. But you must make his kingdom, and uprightness before him, your greatest care, and you will have all these other things besides. So do not worry about tomorrow, for tomorrow will have worries of its own.
>
> Matthew 6:25–34, Goodspeed

Faith in God is the only true security. God never fails, and his love and care for his own never changes. Paul wrote to the Philippians: "my God shall supply all your need according to his riches in glory by Christ Jesus" (9:19). The prayer for daily bread takes God's promises at their face value and is an expression of childlike faith.

V

The Forgiveness of Sins

And forgive us our sins, for we ourselves forgive everyone who is indebted to us.

LUKE 11:4, RSV

And forgive us our debts,
As we also *have forgiven* our debtors . . .

For if you forgive men their trespasses, your heavenly Father also will forgive you; but if you do not forgive men
their trespasses, neither will your Father forgive your trespasses.

MATTHEW 6:12, 14–15, RSV

There are two things that will destroy a Christian's
happiness and usefulness as nothing else: uncon-
fessed and unforgiven sin in one's own life, and a bitter,
stubborn, unforgiving spirit toward another. The two are
inextricably connected in the Model Prayer. As a matter
of fact, Jesus has plainly said that until we have forgiven
everyone who has wronged us, everyone toward whom
we have hatred, resentment, or bitterness, it is useless
for us to ask God to forgive our sins. We cannot have
fellowship with God until we have fellowship with our
brethren. Even our gifts are not acceptable unto him as
long as we and our brothers remain unreconciled.

Clear in my memory is a remarkable experience of
some years ago when I was pastor in an oil-field town
in east Texas. A stalwart young fellow who worked in
the oil field asked me to go with him up into Oklahoma
to see his father, who was sick and was not a professed
Christian. Since the young man himself was not a

church member, his concern for his father's spiritual welfare touched me, and I agreed to go.

It took a good day's driving, and it was almost sundown when we arrived at a typical ranch home nestled among the hills. When I was admitted to the sickroom, I told the sick man the reason for my visit, for I knew that western cattlemen like a straightforward approach. He listened to what I had to say but seemed disturbed about something and asked me to send his son into the room. When the son came out of his father's room, he motioned for me to follow him outside. There, he told me that his father had a brother to whom he had not spoken in twenty years. Now, he wanted to be reconciled to his brother. On the next day, we drove about 150 miles to where the old man's brother lived and brought him back with us.

The brother went into the sickroom. After a long time, he came out wiping his eyes and said that his brother wanted to see me again. I went in, and the old man said, "Preacher, I have wanted to be a Christian for many years, but the foolish quarrel between me and my brother and my stubbornness in waiting for him to make the first move stood in the way. My brother and I are now reconciled, and if you will pray for me, I am ready. If God can forgive my stubborn heart and my many sins . . ." He broke down and could say no more. I prayed, and then he prayed, and God did give him peace and assurance. When we were ready to go back to Texas, he said, "If I never see you again in this life, I'll meet you over yonder, in the place Jesus has gone to prepare." Less than a month later I was called to Oklahoma again to conduct this man's funeral, and to assure his weeping relatives that he died trusting in Jesus.

It may seem to be a hard requirement that you must forgive others *as* you expect God to forgive you, for there are some things that are hard to forgive—and even harder to forget! When we have been wronged, we tend to forget that the burden rests on the offended one as much as it does on the one committing the offense. We should remember that God takes the initiative in forgiving us. He sent his Son to be the propitiation for our sins; he sends the Holy Spirit to make us conscious of our sins and give us the grace to confess and seek forgiveness. It is hard to forgive completely, so as to be free of all bitter memories; but we are told that: "As far as the east is from the west, so far hath [the Lord] removed our transgressions from us" (Psalm 103:12). It was in the light of this quality in the character of God that Jesus taught us to pray,

> Forgive us our debts,
> As we also have forgiven our debtors.

This petition is not conditioned on some future forgiveness but on the fact that we have already forgiven.

Since we cannot have unclouded fellowship with God while we harbor an unforgiving spirit, forgiveness is worth what it costs our pride. "To err is human, to forgive, divine." We may have been wronged, greatly and deliberately. From a human standpoint, we may be justified in demanding our "pound of flesh" by insisting that the wrong be righted or abject apology be made. But in so doing we are insisting that the one who wronged us be bigger and better than we are. Human personality reaches no higher achievement than the ability to forgive freely those who sin against us. If no one hates as much as the person who has committed a wrong, a forgiving spirit still may change that hatred into love.

Remember that upon the cross our Saviour prayed for those who were treating him so cruelly, "Father, forgive them; for they know not what they do." We may not be able, in our own strength, to rid our hearts of bitterness and resentment and hatred. But when we remember what it cost God to reconcile us to himself, we *must*, at whatever cost, be willing to let God cleanse our hearts of these destroyers of our happiness and peace. How tragic it is for the Christian to walk alone in the shadows, with a sore and burdened heart, when he can walk in the light, as God is in the light, while the blood of Jesus Christ continues to cleanse him of all sin and to enable him to have fellowship with God and his fellow Christians.

> This is the charge I keep as mine,
> The goal of every hope and plan—
> To cancel the dividing line
> Between me and my fellow man.
>
> .   .   .   .
>
> More deadly than the blackest art,
> More horror fraught than shell or bomb,
> Hate dims the mind, corrodes the heart
> And strikes the voice of conscience dumb.[1]

In addition to the fact that an unforgiving spirit eats like a cancer in the human personality, we must forgive because we ourselves need forgiveness so much. The fact that a person feels no consciousness of sins, no sense of guilt, no necessity for confession, penitence, or re-

---

[1] From Leslie Pinckney Hill, "My Charge," in *Masterpieces of Religious Verse*, Morrison, *op. cit.*, p. 469; used by permission.

pentance, is not an evidence of a healthy spiritual or moral condition. On the contrary, it may be evidence that one has never experienced regeneration but is still dead in his trespasses and sins. He is not conscious of any rift in his fellowship with God because he has actually not known such fellowship. The nearer one is to God, the clearer is his concept of the holiness of God and the more acute is his consciousness of sins.

When young Isaiah went into the Temple with a sorely burdened heart about the condition of King Uzziah, whom he admired and loved—King Uzziah whose brilliant career ended as a leper—the prophet saw the Lord "high and lifted up." As Isaiah witnessed his glory and majesty, and heard the seraphim singing, he fell on his face and cried: "I am undone; because I am a man of unclean lips, and I dwell in the midst of a people of unclean lips" (Isa. 6:5). When Simon Peter first knew that Christ was God, he cried: "Depart from me; for I am a sinful man, O Lord!" (Luke 5:8). The presence of God always produces a consciousness of sin in man.

John, "the beloved disciple," always close to Jesus in the days of his flesh, expressed the Christian's need for a good relationship with his fellows at the beginning of his first epistle: "That which we have seen and heard we proclaim also to you, so *that you may have fellowship with us;* and our fellowship is with the Father and with his Son Jesus Christ. And we are writing this that our joy may be complete" (1 John 1:3–4, RSV). John's joy could not be complete unless there were fellowship between him and all other Christians, *but his fellowship was with the Father and with his Son Jesus Christ.* So must there be unclouded fellowship with God *and* other Christians.

John went on to deal, more clearly than any other

New Testament writer, with the believer and the problem of sin. Confusion comes when a part of John's message is separated from the whole. Here is his message:

This then is the message which we have heard of him, and declare unto you, that God is light, and in him is no darkness at all. If we say that we have fellowship with him, and walk in darkness, we lie, and do not the truth: but if we walk in the light, as he is in the light, we have fellowship one with another, and the blood of Jesus Christ his Son cleanseth us from all sin (1 John 1:5–7).

Fellowship with God and with one another are considered together, and both rest upon the continual cleansing of the blood. John proceeded to deal with the heresy of perfectionism, "If we say that we have no sin, we deceive ourselves, and the truth is not in us." The Christian who says, "I am done with sin," "I cannot sin," "I am living above sin," is not facing reality but practicing self-deceit. "The truth is not in" those who make such claims. Perfectionism and antinomianism, the heresy that a Christian is no longer bound by the moral law, go hand in hand and are deadly heresies.

The fact that Christians cannot be perfect in the present life does not mean, however, that we must be helpless victims of sin. Thus John went on to write, "If we confess our sins, he is faithful and just to forgive us our sins, and to cleanse us from all unrighteousness. If we say that we have not sinned, we make him a liar, and his word is not in us" (1 John 1:9–10). People who deny their sinfulness contradict God himself, but those who honestly recognize and confess their spiritual need find God ready to forgive and cleanse them. It is thus in the gracious character of God rather than in any sinless character possible for man that our hope for victory over sin lies. Nor is the forgiveness of sins a light matter. Some treat it as such and act as though praying for the forgiveness of sins is no more serious than asking another's pardon for accidentally stepping on his foot. Luther once said that the forgiveness of sin is *"nodus Deo vindice dignus,"* a knot that needs God to unravel. Herrmann has said, "To anyone who really experiences it, forgiveness comes not as a matter of course, but as an astounding revelation of love." [2]

No requirement of God is arbitrary, "fixed by caprice, without adequate determining principle." This surely applies to the requirement that we forgive as we expect to be forgiven. Perhaps God wants to impress upon us that forgiveness is no easy or simple matter. As we search our hearts for our attitude toward those who have offended or wronged us—even by transgressing all the laws of decency and right—we are made more keenly aware of how much it costs a holy God, who cannot look on sin with leniency, to forgive the sinner. Our attitude toward those who have sinned against us is the attitude we can expect God to have toward our sins. Certain it is that we cannot have unclouded fellowship with God until we have fellowship with our fellows. If we are to grow in grace and pray effectively, this prayer, with its necessary corollary, must be part of every prayer.

[2] See T. R. Glover, *Jesus in the Experience of Men* (New York: Association Press, 1921), pp. 71, 86.

VI

Prayer for Moral Guidance and Deliverance

And lead us not into temptation; but deliver us from evil.

LUKE 11:4

Keep us clear of temptation, and save us from evil.

MATTHEW 6:13, PHILLIPS

This petition might well be linked with the fourth Beatitude: "Blessed are they which do hunger and thirst after righteousness: for they shall be filled." The forgiveness of sins, as we have seen, is an essential grace for the Christian, constantly sought in prayer; but this prayer is for the prevention of sin. The forgiveness of sins is the cure for the snake bite; this prayer seeks to keep us out of snake-infested territory. As glorious an experience as the forgiveness of sins is, no one should sin carelessly in order to enjoy it or on the assumption that the sin will be forgiven. In Romans 5:20, Paul wrote, "Where sin abounded, grace did much more abound." Continuing the discussion in the sixth chapter, he asked, "What shall we say then? Shall we continue in sin, that grace may abound? *God forbid.*" J. B. Phillips' *Letters to Young Churches* puts the question dramatically: "Now what is our response to be? Shall we sin to our heart's content and see how far we can exploit the grace of God? What a ghastly thought!" The Christian does not seek sin because he is no longer a captive of sin: Christ

> . . . breaks the *power* of cancelled sin,
> He sets the prisoner free.

CHARLES WESLEY

Why should we pray, "Lead us not into temptation"? Does God ever lead men into temptation?

We read that Jesus, after his baptism, was "led up of the spirit into the wilderness *to be tempted of the devil*" (Matt. 4:2). The word "tempted" means to be tried or to be tested. Such testing may be from a good or a bad motive—certainly it was from a good motive here since the Spirit was leading Jesus. The temptation of Jesus was for a definite purpose. Although Jesus was human as well as divine, he was free from the taint of sin. As the Captain of our salvation, he was made perfect through suffering (Heb. 2:10–18), and as our eternal High Priest who should be touched with a feeling of our infirmities, he had to be "in all points tempted like as we are, yet without sin" (Heb. 4:15). In the very beginning of his public ministry as the promised Messiah, it was necessary that he should meet Satan in mortal combat, feeling in his flesh the strength of Satan's wiles and demonstrating his power against all that the power of darkness could devise.

God was testing the faith of Abraham when he commanded him to offer Isaac, "the son of promise," as a sacrifice. But God quickly showed him a way out when Abraham had proved his faith—to himself; God knew Abraham's faith already.

God *permitted* Satan to try Job, but God knew Job's faith.

Jesus said to Peter: "Satan hath desired to have you, that he may sift you as wheat: but I have prayed for thee, that thy faith fail not: and when thou art converted [not *if* but *when*], strengthen thy brethren" (Luke 22:31–32).

All of these facts do not weaken the declaration of James: "Let no man say when he is tempted, I am tempted of God: for God cannot be tempted *with evil,* neither tempteth he any man [with evil]: But every man is tempted, when he is drawn away of his own lust, and enticed." James 1:12–15 is not so likely to be confusing if it is remembered that there is a transition from the use of "temptation" in verse 12, meaning "testing," to a discussion of the problem of being "tempted with evil" in verses 13–15.

Why should one seek to avoid temptation? Does not one gain moral strength by exposing himself to temptations and resisting them? The idea that it is better to meet every sort of temptation and learn its power— even to sin in order to learn from experience that "sin doesn't pay"—is as productive of human degradation as any philosophy that ever crawled from the slimy underpinnings of the abode of the father of lies!

The philosophy of "realism" that revels in knowing about "life" in all its sordid and morbid possibilities is responsible for a flood of pornographic "literature," describing in detail the thrills of illicit sexual intercourse in a way that would probably have brought a blush to the cheek of a hardened prostitute of a generation ago. Today this is read avidly by shockproof boys and girls in high school, and discussed around the bridge tables by the "gentler sex." One can hardly go into a drugstore in any city, town, village, or hamlet in America without passing a rack filled with cheap, paperback novels whose theme, if correctly portrayed by the suggestive scenes and indecent exposure of the human anatomy on the covers, is lurid and filthy lust. These have now invaded grocery stores and the "five-and-tens." Young America, and old America as well, is being systematically and constantly challenged to test the thrill of illicit "love." This is certainly not a blanket indictment of all paperback publishers, for many of them have made good literature available to the masses at prices they can afford. Nor is it excusing the higher-priced books that throw in a bedroom scene every dozen or so pages in order to "flavor" the uninteresting stuff in between.

Nor is that the worst: so-called "comic" books that abound in all sorts of crime, horror, and perversion, pictured in great detail for those not yet old enough to read or understand the pornographic novel, are everywhere available. They are even welcomed by some parents and teachers whose sole concern is to keep children quiet and out of mischief! My heart quails often as I see groups of children sitting on the floor in front of the comic book rack, avidly sampling those they do not buy, absolutely lost to their surroundings. From the "comics" one can learn the technique of robbing a bank, kidnaping a baby, blowing up a bridge, setting a house afire, and killing another person with gun, knife, poison, or garrote. A famous detective strip in the daily papers gives a postgraduate course in crime. The criminal is usually an unpleasant and unattractive person whose looks and name point up his perversion, and he is always punished—usually by being shot. Yet the way the crime is committed is pictured in such detail, with diagrams, that it remains in the mind. The public seems too indifferent to do anything about such things as these.

Certainly this is not an argument that "ignorance is bliss," nor is it a plea for a return to stories of fairy princes and princesses and of heroes and heroines who are too good for this world. Nor is it an argument that parents should rear their children in an atmosphere of deceit and make-believe, nor that the wholesome truths about life, including sex, should be treated as hush-hush.

Quite the contrary! The parent and teacher should give much thought and prayer to the effort of presenting the real "facts of life" to children much earlier in our modern age than was heretofore thought necessary. But I do insist, and God's Word insists, that the emphasis should be upon the good, and the pure, and the beautiful. "Whatsoever things are *true*, whatsoever things are *honest*, whatsoever things are *just*, whatsoever things are *pure*, whatsoever things are *lovely*, whatsoever things are *of good report*; if there be any virtue, and if there be any praise, *think on these things*" (Phil. 4:8). Or, as this verse is given in the translation of J. B. Phillips: "If you believe in goodness and if you value the approval of God, fix your minds on the things which are holy and right and pure and beautiful and good." For "as [a man] thinketh in his heart, so is he" (Prov. 23:7).

Much modern literature, of the sort just described, is no more a true picture of life than is a cesspool a picture of all bodies of water. The less we know about evil, except that it is evil, the better our chances of remaining pure and wholesome and strong. Certainly the less we *think* on evil, the better off we are. When Eve was tempted to look at the forbidden fruit, Satan caused her to believe that it was desirable *to make one wise* (i.e., sophisticated). The whole idea is from Satan.

In our day, parents are urged not to teach their children to be abstainers, for "beer belongs" and alcoholic beverages are essential to "men of distinction" and women of charm. To advocates of this philosophy, the only problem is in learning "how to handle liquor" and knowing "when to quit." Meanwhile insane asylums, sanitariums, and hospitals are totally unable to care for the increasing flood of alcoholics, and this "sophisticated" attitude is largely responsible. It is also helping to ruin lives, break up homes, and baptize our highways with the blood of often innocent victims of the drunken driver. It is helping to fill the hearts of men and women with vain and bitter regrets that must be drowned in ever-increasing doses of the scourge of humanity. Alcoholism is a disease—but it has never yet attacked a total abstainer.

Do not be deceived. To pray, "Lead us not into temptation," is not to pray to be isolated from life, to live in an ivory tower, to withdraw into a monastery, or to live as a hermit. But praying thus does mean that one seeks to direct his thinking and his daily walk into right paths and that he chooses his intimate associates from among those who also avoid evil.

When I was a very young man, I went to the city of Dallas to attend business "college." I had bought my "scholarship," but it was necessary for me to work for my room and board. For a time, I was too busy getting into the swing of study and doing my outside work to get into trouble. In those days, there was a saloon in practically every block—this was the era of the five-cent beer and free lunch—and the city was honeycombed with cheap upstairs "hotels" and fancier brothels. After a while, an older man, who had been out of school so long that he was rusty on arithmetic and spelling, offered to pay my rent if I would share a room with him and help him with his homework. At the same time, a job in a lunchroom from ten until two gave me three meals a day and a little spending money.

On Sunday, taking advantage of my new freedom, I went to church, "as my custom was." After attending a Sunday school class of young men taught by a famous lawyer and hearing Dr. George W. Truett preach, I united with the church on promise of a letter. At Baptist

Young People's Union that evening, I received an invitation to a social to be given in the church basement the following Friday. I moved in with my new-found friend on Monday and attended the social on Friday, where I met some of the finest young people in Dallas.

It was on Saturday night that my roommate suggested we "make the rounds" of the more respectable brothels, merely for the fun of it. He was "wise" in the ways of the world and "knew the ropes." These houses had once been respectable dwellings but were now dark and lonesome-looking from the outside, with blinds tightly drawn. I was assured that they were quite different inside. It was a temptation, but the pattern of my social and recreational life had been set by the influence of a church that cared for its young people and for "the stranger within the gates."

The second part of this petition, "but deliver us from evil," is quite as necessary as the first, for no matter how circumspect our behavior, no matter how guarded our walk, or how careful our choice of companions, temptations are inevitable. The sins of which we have been speaking are, largely, the sins of the flesh. There are sins of the spirit, of the mind, of the heart quite as dangerous and destructive to the personality, and quite as reprehensible as the sins of fleshly indulgence. It is worthy of note that Jesus showed pity and compassion for the victims of fleshly lusts and demon-possession, while his bitterest indictment was reserved for the proud, haughty, self-righteous hypocrites who thought of themselves as "the" people of God. Temptations are inevitable because we are sinful by nature and because we live in an evil environment.

In the previous chapter, we noted that John wrote, "If we say that we have no sin, we deceive ourselves, and the truth is not in us." Remember that John was writing to believers. The doctrine of sinless perfection is a delusion and a lie. Through justification by faith the *guilt* of sin is removed, the penalty paid in full, and we are just before God. In regeneration we have been born "from above," have become "partakers of the divine nature," and are "a new creation"; but the old Adam is not completely eradicated. There is a law in our members that must constantly be kept in subjection. Paul, writing to the Philippian Christians out of the maturity of Christian faith, said, "Not as though I had already attained, either were already perfect: but I . . . press toward the mark" (Phil. 3:12, 14). Again: "Let him that thinketh he standeth take heed lest he fall" (1 Cor. 10:12).

No one needs this admonition more than the Christian minister whom God has endowed with many pleasing gifts and who, through powerful friends, fortuitous circumstances, or even the favor of God, is elevated to a place of prominence, where he is showered with compliments, praise, and adulation. Spiritual pride, a haughty spirit, a pharisaical self-righteousness, a "holier-than-thou" attitude has ruined the sweetness and power of many a man who might have been great rather than merely popular. Just so, the sins that ruin many a Christian are often not the easily recognized sins of the flesh, but a worldly spirit, a selfish ambition for personal aggrandizement, love of luxury and wealth, a desire to stand in the spotlight, love of ease, and an avoidance of the cross.

Then, there is no perfect environment on this earth. Recently an experienced, thoughtful, consecrated speaker at an evangelistic conference said that if the members of his church were as faithful in attending the worship services as the devil is, he would need to double the capacity of his church building. He said that the devil often sat by his side and whispered in his ear before the sermon, urging that what he felt impelled to say would not be good policy, neither safe nor wise, and that he should soften his message, or, at least, be pleasantly vague. A well-known theological professor, now deceased, once said in class that if he were looking for the world's greatest sinner, he would not search in the dives and places of sin that infest our cities, but in some place such as a theological seminary—because sin against the light, and in spite of opportunity, is greater than sin committed in dark ignorance or weakness.

I thought in my boyhood that if I could attend a revival meeting all the time, I would never fall into temptation. I thought that once I secured the courage and faith to answer the call to become a preacher, no more temptations would ever have any appeal. Such a false idea—based upon ignorance of human nature, of the powers of evil, and of the Word of God—is responsible for monasteries and convents. By withdrawing from the world, men and women have believed that they could escape from temptation and achieve holiness. Jesus prayed: "I pray not that thou shouldest take them out of the world, but that thou shouldest keep them from the evil" (John 17:15). We live out our lives "in the midst of a crooked and perverse nation" (Phil. 2:15), said Paul, who commanded us to live as children of God, shining like lights in the darkness and holding forth the Word of life.

Enduring temptation is a part of our Christian experience. James said, "My brethren, count it all joy when ye *fall* [not walk] into divers temptations; knowing this, that the trying of your faith worketh patience" (1:13–14). J. B. Phillips has put James's admonition

thus: "When all kinds of trials and temptations crowd
into your lives, my brothers, don't resent them as in-
truders, but welcome them as friends! Realise that they
come to test your faith and to produce in you the quality
of endurance." Here temptations are regarded as tests
of faith. It may be that James was talking about *trials,*
rather than temptations to sin, unless grumbling at our
"hard lot" is sin! However, we are warned to be on our
guard constantly against all the wiles of the evil one.
For we have to struggle not with blood and flesh, but
with spiritual forces of evil. We must put on God's
armor and *hold our ground,* praying at all times in the
Spirit with all manner of prayer and entreaty (see Eph.
6:12–18).

So we need God's deliverance from the forces of evil,
even when we stand fully equipped in all the panoply of
a Christian warrior. If evil always appeared in its true
guise, the earnest Christian would have little trouble
resisting it. Even Satan himself, however, sometimes appears as an "angel of light." "Let your conscience be
your guide," must be one of the devil's favorite proverbs.
There are certain categorical imperatives that no man
can violate with impunity unless he has destroyed his
last vestige of human feeling by continued sin; but our
consciences are influenced by early training, our ev-
eryday associates, our environment, and other factors. Conscience also may become seared by sin. Every
person who is honest knows that things which once gave
him a sharp twinge of conscience may come through repeated practice to be defended with a clear or, at least,
an inactive conscience. God's eternal law, not the stand-
ards of any age, culture, civilization, or social group, is
the norm of Christian conduct.

Again, conscience often does not operate until the

thing is done. That which appeared at first as innocent pastime or, at the worst, a violation of outmoded "convention" is seen in retrospect as the sin that it is. Therefore, constant prayer for divine guidance is essential that we may discern between good and evil, and be able to reject the evil. "If any of you lack wisdom, let him ask of God, that giveth to all men liberally, and upbraideth not" (James 1:5).

Neither the weakness of the flesh nor the influence of an evil environment is to be regarded as an *excuse* for sin. When David wrote, "Behold, I was shapen in iniquity; and in sin did my mother conceive me," he was not offering an excuse for his sin but recognizing his deep need for God's cleansing grace. We are not to say, "God made me thus, and I am only doing 'that which comes naturally,' " in extenuation of sin. God did not make us thus; sin did. "When I am weak," Paul said, "then am I strong." When he realized his weakness, he was armed for the fray and felt the need of divine aid.

In conclusion, and as an incentive to this prayer, *God has promised deliverance in the hour of temptation.* "There hath no temptation taken you but such as is common to man" (1 Cor. 10:13). You are not so different as you think you are. We are not the victims of superhuman temptations, for "God is faithful, and he will not let you be tempted beyond your strength."

Listen!

God does not turn his children loose to be the unprotected prey of all the imps of hell! God does not leave us alone to fight superhuman powers! We "are kept by the power of God unto salvation ready to be revealed [in all its glorious perfection] in the last time" (1 Peter 1:5).

Consider Job. There is a great deal of comfort in the

book of Job. This is not because of Job's patience or his ability to say, "The Lord gave, and the Lord hath taken away; blessed be the name of the Lord" (1:22). These words *could* be used to express a deadly and paralyzing fatalism, amounting to indifference. Where I get the most comfort is from the fact that *God set a limit beyond which Satan could not go!*

Satan had challenged Job's righteousness by saying, in effect: "Job is not serving you for nothing. He is serving you for what he can get out of it. You have given him wealth, blessed him, and built a fence around him and his. Take away what he has, and he'll turn against you."

God answered: "Behold, all that he hath is in thy power; *only upon himself put not forth thine hand.*"

Terrible, unexpected, and inexplicable were the tragedies that descended upon Job in rapid succession. But *he remained faithful.* Satan was not convinced: "Touch his bone and his flesh, and he will curse thee to thy face."

God answered: "He is in thine hand; *but save his life*" (2:6). Thus far, Satan, but no farther!

He "will not suffer you to be tempted above that ye are able [thanks be unto God!]; but will *with the temptation* also make a way to escape, that ye may be able to bear it." There is a way out. So Jesus has taught us to pray: "Deliver us from evil" [or "the evil one"].

VII

Intercessory Prayer for
Lost Humanity

He said unto them, Which of you shall have a friend, and shall go unto him at midnight, and say unto him, Friend, lend me three loaves; For a friend of mine in his journey is come to me, and I have nothing to set before him? And he from within shall answer and say, Trouble me not: the door is now shut, and my children are with me in bed; I cannot rise and give thee. I say unto you, Though he will not rise and give him, because he is his friend, yet because of his importunity he will rise and give him as many as he needeth.

LUKE 11:5–8

This parable of the embarrassed host follows the Model Prayer and is part of Jesus' response to the request, "Lord, teach us to pray."

Intercession naturally had a large place in the prayer life of Jesus. As one reads the seventeenth chapter of John's Gospel, he feels that he is ushered into the very holy of holies of Jesus' communion with the Father. In the first five verses that prayer deals with Jesus himself and his ministry, but the rest is for his followers, whom he is to leave in the world as sheep surrounded by wolves. It is his high-priestly prayer. In that prayer he says: "I pray for them: I pray not for the world" (17:9). But a little later he includes "them also which shall believe on me through their word." The risen Christ, at the right hand of God, makes continual intercession for us, for he is High Priest, as well as King.

One cannot read the poignant words, "O Jerusalem, Jerusalem, killing the prophets and stoning those who

are sent to you! How often would I have gathered your
children together as a hen gathers her brood under her
wings, and you would not!" nor hear from the parched
lips of the dying Saviour the prayer for his tormentors,
"Father, forgive them; for they know not what they do!"
without being assured that Jesus prayed for sinners. He
commanded his disciples to "pray for those who . . .
persecute you" or abuse you.

The ministry of intercession, which must be a part of
the prayer life of every Christian, is twofold: (1) prayer
for lost men—for all who do not know our Saviour, and
for unsaved individuals—and (2) prayer for the household of faith—for one another, for those who preach the
Word, for missionaries and others that work for Christ
and his kingdom. This parable of the embarrassed host
teaches, I believe, intercession for lost humanity.

Only one who has a keen sense of hospitality can fully
appreciate the embarrassment of the host in this story,
the desperate urgency that sent him to disturb his neighbor at midnight and persist until his request would be
granted. We miss the point of the story almost alto-
gether if we interpret "a friend of mine" to mean an intimate acquaintance whose visit was expected or one to
whom the situation could be explained. Someone had
come to his house at midnight, off his road, lost, hungry,
and tired to the bone. It is likely that he was a complete stranger whose only claim upon the host was his
desperate need and that he had asked for shelter and
food. In this day of motels, tourist courts, roadside
parks, and restaurants at frequent intervals, we know
little about the customs of hospitality that prevailed in
more primitive times and in the pioneer days of our own
country.

Years ago I was pastor of a rural church in western

Texas, about twenty miles off a highway. Once on my way home in a "T model" Ford, with my wife and baby girl, I was overtaken by a typical Texas blizzard and by darkness—at about the same time. We had just turned off the graveled highway into the country lane when the car stuck in the mud. The roads had been dragged and the mudholes smoothed over. After about an hour's work with prize pole and brush put under the wheels, we got on our way. The wind was rising steadily and the thermometer dropping rapidly. We stuck again and managed to get on our way after much toil. Thoughts of having to spend the night in a mudhole did nothing to relieve my feeling of tension over the uncertain road.

The third time the wheels sank into the black ooze to the axles happened just after we had passed a dark farmhouse near the road and had noticed smoke coming out of the chimney. I opened the drain on the radiator, and we walked back to the house. My call brought an instant response: a lamp was lighted, the door was opened wide, and we went in. By the time I could tell of our plight, the fire that had been banked for the night was replenished, children were changed into other beds, and a bed was prepared for us. I shall never forget the luxury of that warm bed, or the relief I felt, or the breakfast that was ready when we awoke. After a leisurely breakfast, the farmer and his sons went with me to the car. The ground was solidly frozen around the wheels, but we chopped them free. Then one of the boys arrived with a team of mules to pull the car to solid ground. To have offered to pay would have been a violation of Western hospitality on my part. We had been strangers, but now we were friends. I remembered the poem "The House by the Side of the Road" and applied it to this farm family.

In Jesus' parable, we may first see a comprehension of human need. One cannot, of course, have very much concern for lost humanity unless he knows that men are lost. The doctrine our fathers called "total depravity" is very unpopular today. Humanism sees man as a sort of knight in shining armor, struggling with natural forces that are neither friendly nor unfriendly, lifting himself unaided from the muck to glowing heights of civilization, culture, and moral achievement. The modernistic conception of sin is that it is a sort of "growing pain," a mistake that man makes as he seeks to adjust to life. Such ideas have made the concept of "total depravity" unpopular.

However, one who is to be a winner of souls must at least know that men are lost and that only God can save them. The deadly virus of sin is in the blood stream of the race, a part of our human heritage since the fall. There is but one Physician who can heal, and the only remedy is *a blood transfusion*—the blood that was shed on Calvary. We may "enlist" people in "church work" to whom it will be said at the judgment, "I never knew you"; but if we are to get men and women into the kingdom of God, we must know how one is delivered from the kingdom of darkness into the kingdom of light. There are far too many "do-gooders" in the world who are not serving as ambassadors for Christ and far too few evangelists who are urging men to be reconciled to God.

Let us look at the condition of the man whose need motivated the action in this parable. Jesus said that he was "off the road" (*ex hodou*). That expression has usually been taken to mean merely that he was taking a journey, yet the meaning of the preposition suggests that possibly he had lost his way. If this was what the Lord had in mind, then certainly the condition of the traveler paralleled that of lost people, for they are truly "off the road." They are off the straight and narrow way that leads to life and are walking on the broad way that leads to destruction. This broad way is often a "way which seems right to a man, but its end is the way to death" (Prov. 16:25, RSV). It may be the path of worldly pleasure that leads through the desert of disillusionment, across the rocks of futility to the cliffs of despair. *Men and women have lost the way to happiness in the search for pleasure.* There is only One who can rescue them, and we are his ambassadors.

Many have lost sight of the spiritual and the eternal in their obsession for the things that are temporal and material. They are hard and self-sufficient, often possessing wealth and social distinction. They seem to enjoy life and to feel that they are superior. Too often such people are overlooked by Christian workers, or even worse, they are sought merely for the financial support or the social prominence they could give the church. They are not, perhaps, great sinners in the eyes of men. Yet their personal energies have been diverted to serve merely selfish ends. *They have traded their birthright to the things that are eternal for the things that are only temporal*—and unsatisfying. They have worshiped self rather than God. "I" has become the center of their universe. They, too, have lost the way.

Others have followed false philosophy and vain deceit—intellectuals who are not intelligent, because they ignore him who said: "I am the . . . truth," and leave out of their calculations the supreme Fact of the universe. Others have found a sort of self-hypnosis in one or another of the esoteric cults, the false faiths which use the names of "Christ" and "Christian" but pervert or ignore Christ's teachings.

But does it matter how or why they have lost the way —whether it was through a wrong environment, or unworthy ideals learned in home or school, or some psychological "twist"? Does it matter whether they left the road by deliberate choice or merely drifted? The important thing is that they are lost and that Jesus said, "The Son of man is come to seek and to save that which was lost" (Luke 19:10). He also said, "As thou hast sent me into the world, even so have I also sent them into the world" (John 17:18). You and I, like Paul, are "debtor both to the Greeks, and to the Barbarians; both to the wise, and to the unwise" (Rom. 1:14).

The man in Jesus' parable was hungry. So urgent was his need that, although it was then midnight, he could not wait until morning. There is too much physical hunger in the world, the hunger for a bare diet that will sustain life. We do not know much about that here in America, and God forbid that we ever should. There is something terribly wrong in a world where little children die of hunger or lie whining in the streets with thin limbs and bloated stomachs, while others gorge themselves with meat and waste that which would give life to the hungry. There is something wrong in a world where mountains of food are destroyed or stored up to spoil in one nation while other nations starve. Ships can be found to transport the sinews of war—why not food for the starving millions? Some object that that would disrupt the world's economy! Any economy that can coldly condemn children to death by starvation needs to be disrupted. Unless something is done, and done soon, a day of judgment must come—and it is terrible to contemplate.

But the world has other hungers. There is hunger for human companionship, understanding, sympathy, love. There is the need to know that somebody cares, the need for

> A hand upon your shoulder
> In a friendly sort of way.

That hunger, I am convinced, causes many to go astray.

A deeper hunger cannot be satisfied by human resources: a yearning for the divine Companion. Augustine said: "Thou hast made us for thyself, and our souls are restless until they rest in Thee." [1] There is a thirst that can only be satisfied with the Water of life, and a hunger abated only by the Bread of life. Many are driven by this hunger to seek in strange places for queer substitutes that can never satisfy. They need a friend to introduce them to him who said: "I am the bread of life; he who comes to me shall not hunger, and he who believes in me shall never thirst" (John 6:35, RSV).

The traveler in Jesus' parable also suggests the belatedness of humanity. "At midnight"—that is as late as it can get! A cartoonist recently pictured a clock, with the hands standing at five minutes to midnight and the caption, "It may be later than you think!" It was a sobering and terrifying thought. Have we somehow lost the sense of urgency that marked those New Testament Christians? It has been said that they were expecting the immediate return of the Lord and thus were mistaken. Is any Christian generation mistaken in expecting that Christ might return at any time? Who among us

---

[1] *Confessions*, Bk. I, Chap. I.

would say complacently, "My Lord delayeth his coming" (Luke 12:45)? It may be later than we think for the world. All about us are evidences of "men's hearts failing them for fear, and for looking after those things which are coming on the earth" (Luke 21:26). But whether Christ's return be near or in the distant future, the urgency of the Christian evangelistic task is not lessened. Men are dying every moment of every hour and slipping out into eternity to meet the God they do not know. Others stand on the brink of moral and spiritual disaster, needing a helping hand, a word of caution or encouragement, but above all, *a word of faith.*

In addition to a comprehension of human need, the parable shows a recognition of human inadequacy: "I have nothing to set before him!" The host had done all that he could, explored all his resources, given what he had, or else his going to his friend at midnight would have been an imposition. James has asked, according to J. B. Phillips' translation, "If a fellow man or woman has no clothes to wear and nothing to eat, and one of you say, 'Good luck to you, I hope you'll keep warm and find enough to eat,' and yet give them nothing to meet their physical needs, what on earth is the good of that?" (2:15–16).

But when we have done all that we can do to minister to humanity's need, we must call upon God. No human can save a soul from sin: not by psychoanalysis, counseling, or guidance; not by "brain-washing"; not by scolding or giving advice. Our scolding and analyzing must bring a conviction of sin, and our counseling and advice must point the way to Jesus. We have to say, "Behold the Lamb of God, which taketh away the sin of the world." Only God can forgive sins. Only God can make the sinner clean. Only God can give new life and "the peace . . . which passeth understanding." The minister should avail himself of all that modern psychiatry has to offer in dealing with troubled souls; but as a "physician of souls," he must be a man of prayer, a man of faith, a man thoroughly grounded in the doctrine of grace. Otherwise, the final result may be an "adjusted" pagan rather than a child of God.

Then, the parable suggests a sense of divine sufficiency. "Friend, lend me three loaves"—not "See if you can find a loaf of bread." We can always turn to God in the same confidence with which the host in the parable turned to his neighbor. God's larder is always full. When the disciples had failed to heal the demon-possessed lad, the father of the boy said to Jesus: "If you can do anything, have pity on us and help us." Jesus replied: "If you can! All things are possible to him who believes" (Mark 9:22–23, RSV). Do we believe that "he is *able* also to save them to the uttermost that come unto God by him" (Heb. 7:25)? Do we actually believe that "Christ is the answer"—the answer to humanity's problems, the supply for humanity's need, the Physician who can heal humanity's hurt? There must be conviction—as deep as life itself, conviction tested in our own experience—that God does have both wisdom and power and that it is his desire "that all should come to repentance" (2 Pet. 3:9). God can reach where we cannot touch, go where our earth-bound feet cannot go, understand where we can only grope for an answer, and heal where we can find no remedy.

Finally, the understanding of humanity's need, compassion for that need, and a conviction of divine sufficiency, must lead to a dedication to the task of intercession. "Because of his importunity"—we shall notice the problem of interpreting this phrase in the chapter on

"The Persistence of Faith." Suffice it to say here that the needed quality is a concern for others and a conviction of divine sufficiency that does not give up easily. If we question the necessity for importunity, we may as well question the necessity for praying at all. God is certainly as much interested in the salvation of the lost as we are. He sent his only begotten Son to "taste death for every man" (Heb. 2:9). He is "not willing that any should perish, but that all should come to repentance" (2 Peter 3:9).

However, God has made us partners in the work of redemption, and it is his plan that we should share in the "quest for souls." What sort of partners does he want? Suppose we act on the assumption that when we ask God to save a lost friend or loved one, he either acts immediately or else he will not act at all? Would not our intercessory prayer be as meaningless and careless as the phrase, often heard in public prayer, "Save the lost"? There would be no necessity for deep concern, for persistent importunity. We would merely make a list of those we wanted saved, read the list to God, and go blithely upon our way. Or, to carry the idea to the point of absurdity, we could pray daily: "Save the heathen— the people of China, Japan, India, Africa, the islands of the sea," and relieve ourselves and our churches of the necessity and expense of missionary work.

Such an attitude would be in strange contrast to the attitude of Paul expressed in his letter to the Romans: "Brethren, my heart's desire and prayer to God for Israel is, that they might be saved" (10:1). "I say the truth in Christ, I lie not, my conscience also bearing me witness in the Holy Ghost, That I have great heaviness and continual sorrow in my heart. *For I could wish that myself were accursed from Christ* for my brethren, my kinsmen according to the flesh" (9:1–3). Likewise, Moses asked God to spare Israel or: "If not, blot me, I pray thee, out of thy book which thou hast written" (Ex. 32:32). More than once this intrepid man stood in the breach. God assured him, "I have pardoned according to thy word" (Num. 14:20). Paul, in the wonderful third chapter of Philippians, expressed an aspiration to know "the fellowship of his sufferings" or "the partnership of his passion."

One who shares the concern of Paul or the responsibility Moses felt for Israel or the passion of Jesus for the lost cannot easily desist from intercession until he has the answer in his heart, until the lost friend is saved. God wants us to be enough in earnest to persevere and have sufficient faith for importunity. When our prayers are not immediately answered, we are to go on seeking and knocking and asking.

When Henry Weldon and I were students in Burleson College, he conducted a revival in a country church. In a day service only a small group had assembled, for the weather was threatening. Instead of preaching, he had called for testimonies and requests for prayer. He noticed that a man, who had been plowing in a field near the church, slipped into the vestibule out of a sudden rain, unseen by anyone else. A woman stood up. After a struggle to regain her composure, she said, "I have been asking this church every summer for forty years to pray for my husband. He is a good man and a good husband, but he isn't a Christian. I haven't the courage or the faith to ask you again. It must be that God does not intend to save him, although I have prayed for him daily."

She sat down, and there was a sudden commotion in the back of the church. The man who had come in out of the rain, dressed in his work clothes and unshaven, came stumbling down the aisle. "Wife, don't say that! For forty years I have depended upon your prayers as my only hope. I always intended to make my peace with God some day. But if you lose faith . . . please pray for me! And the rest of you, pray for me now, that I might be saved today." They did, and he was—after forty years!

"Ask, and it shall be given you; seek, and ye shall find; knock, and it shall be opened unto you" (Luke 11:9). Cling to the promise, but keep on asking, seeking, knocking, with faith in the power and love of God. The answer will come. Or if the person for whom you are praying resists all appeals, you still will have shared the compassion of Christ, who "died for all."

VIII

The Ministry of Intercession

(for the Work of the Kingdom
and the Household of Faith)

In the previous chapter we studied the teaching of Jesus regarding intercessory prayer for the lost, as illustrated by the parable of the embarrassed host. We consider now the teachings of Jesus regarding the ministry of intercession for the work of the kingdom and for others in the household of faith. In doing so, we need to remember that Jesus taught both by precept and example and that the Gospels do not contain a record of all that Jesus did and taught (cf. John 20: 30–31). For example, Acts 20:35 records a saying of Jesus that Paul quoted which does not appear in any of the Gospels.

There are two statements in the recorded sayings of Jesus that teach intercessory prayer for the work and workers of the kingdom. The Lord said, "Pray ye therefore the Lord of the harvest, that he will send forth labourers into his harvest" (Matt. 9:38). Also the words in the Model Prayer, "Thy Kingdom come. Thy will be done on earth, as it is in heaven," teach us to pray that his kingdom shall spread throughout the earth and into every area of life until God's perfect will is done in all the earth. That prayer certainly includes all the workers of the kingdom: that they may be true and faithful, that they may receive wisdom and power for the task, that they may be preserved from harm in order to do the work, and that their work may be effective.

Also relevant is the promise, "If two of you shall agree on earth as touching any thing that they shall ask, it shall be done for them of my Father which is in heaven" (Matt. 18:19). Here is a group, of any size from two up, which covenants together to pray for something that is of such absorbing interest and vital concern that all are in perfect accord concerning it. We may safely infer that each member of the group is praying for every other member, since the object of their prayer thus binds them together.

The example of Jesus' own life of intercession can be seen in his statement to Peter that Satan had demanded that he might sift him as wheat: "But I have prayed for thee, that thy faith fail not: and when thou art converted, strengthen thy brethren" (Luke 22:32). The seventeenth chapter of John records in detail Jesus' prayer for his own. This must have been the burden of much of his secret prayer all during his earthly ministry. We are taught that Jesus, as our eternal High Priest in the real holy of holies makes continual intercession for us (cf. Heb. 7:25). Paul put great emphasis upon Christians praying for each other. Not only did he express appreciation of the prayers that had been offered in his behalf, but he insisted that "supplications, prayers, *intercessions*, and giving of thanks, be made for all men; [especially] for kings, and for all that are in authority; that we may lead a quiet and peaceable life in all godliness and honesty" (1 Tim. 2:1–2). We may safely infer that the Christian tradition in New Testament times put great value upon the ministry of intercession. Every believer is a priest of God, with priestly access to the throne of grace, and the chief business of a priest is intercession.

Among other things, Christian work suffers from two great evils: There are not enough workers for the many tasks that need to be done, and there are too many who are trying to do the work of the kingdom whom the Lord has not chosen or called. These either lack the moral or spiritual evidences of a "vocation," or they are not *where* the Lord wants them to be. To the first statement every pastor and educational director and every mission board secretary will instantly agree. The burden of every pastor of a modern church is to find enough workers for the many jobs to be done. Oftentimes he is driven to accept anyone who will take the place, whether it is to teach a Sunday school class, lead a young people's organization, play the piano, or sing in the choir. He knows that there are people in his church, if he stays long enough in one church to know his flock, who are eminently qualified in every respect—except a willing spirit and a dedicated life. They could do the work that is to be done gloriously, if they could be persuaded to do it.

Probably we have not put the importance of work for the kingdom upon a high enough plane. "Church work" does not seem to be of very great importance to many who will readily accept places of responsibility in social and community projects. *The fault is ours.* Instead of regarding the smallest place in church work as of such importance that only the Lord can select and call and appoint one to the task, the pastor and the educational director must beg and cajole anyone they can get to undertake the work. Let the church make the needs of the harvest field the burden of its prayers and recognize that God calls every worker who is qualified for the task. Let each member pray with a willingness to accept whatever responsibility the Lord may lay upon him. Then, there will be workers for every task that comes as a commission from the Lord of the harvest.

Hallesby, in his wonderful book *Prayer,* has suggested that we not only pray that the Lord send forth workers but also that none be sent except God send them. He wrote, "There are people on the foreign mission fields who should never have been there. Some of them have not even been converted to God. And at the same time there are people here at home who should have been missionaries. This is our own fault." [1] The same is true, he added, of pastors, teachers, and leaders.

Once when I was holding a series of revival meetings in east Texas rural churches, an old Negro, riding a mule without a saddle, came by the place where I had been entertained. His hair and beard were white as snow, and there was an innate dignity in his bearing, not affected by his worn clothing or plebian method of transportation. My host told me the old Negro was a preacher of the gospel. He could neither read nor write, but if someone read a passage of Scripture to him he could repeat it word for word. I wanted to meet him. He told me about his conversion and call, and about his work among his people. Then he said, "I talks to de Lawd, and de Lawd talks to me. He says to me one day: 'When you sees a man going down de road wid a Bible under his arm—I ain't put 'em all out.' " I have never forgotten it, for the Lord had told me the same thing.

"We are ambassadors for Christ." In the foreign service of every great nation there are career men and dedicated men, although those technically called "career men" include many truly dedicated men. The latter are

---

[1] O. Hallesby, *Prayer* (tr. Clarence J. Carlsen; Minneapolis: Augsburg Publishing House, 1931), p. 74.

often looked on as queer ducks, radical in their views, and liable to cause trouble. Career men are interested supremely in their own advancement. Every decision and judgment is colored by whether or not a thing is popular with the powers that be. The question is constantly in their minds: "What effect will this decision have upon my career?" The dedicated men are supremely concerned with the welfare and prestige of their country, and the peace of the world. They are sometimes shelved into some innocuous position while bright young opportunists are advanced. I am sorry to say that it is my conviction that there are far too many "career men" in Christian pulpits and places of denominational leadership. *Only dedicated men can render the highest service to the kingdom of Christ.*

Dr. George W. Truett, as a young schoolteacher, lived in his father's home in Whitewright, Texas. A group of deacons in the Whitewright church decided that the Lord was calling George into the ministry. They prayed that he would respond to the call. One Saturday in 1890, at the regular church conference, the oldest deacon made a motion that the church call a presbytery and ordain Brother George W. Truett to the full work of the gospel ministry. Dr. Truett protested, then asked them to wait six months, but the deacon insisted the church had been called to do this, and that they dared not wait. On the next day he was examined and ordained, and as he told the story of God's dealing with him, one of the worst men in the community was converted. The world owes a debt of gratitude to that group of praying deacons. They took literally the command of Jesus to pray that the Lord of the harvest send laborers into his harvest, and helped young Truett answer the call.

If Christ's churches took the fellowship of his compassion for the needy harvest field as seriously as they should, they would pray earnestly and constantly that the Lord would call and send forth workers from their midst. There would be enough dedicated men and women for the task. Not only so, but the spiritual demands of such praying congregations upon their leaders and teachers would be such that only those who have unmistakably been called of God would have spiritual resources sufficient to assume places of responsibility. It is my conviction that God not only calls men into specific kinds of service but directs and leads them to their fields of service. Many churches in selecting a pastor search for the sort of man they want rather than praying that the Lord's man for the place be found.

After we have prayed for the Lord to send forth laborers into his harvest, is our work of intercession finished? Not at all. Those of us to whom the Lord has committed this blessed ministry should sustain these workers with our prayers, as Aaron and Hur held up the arms of Moses on the hill in Rephidim while Joshua fought the Amalekites.

We should *pray* for our pastors.

The work of a true pastor is not easy, even in a small congregation. It is more difficult in some ways in a small church than in a large one, for the members expect more individual attention. The pastor must be both prophet and priest. He must "reprove, rebuke, exhort with all longsuffering and doctrine" (2 Tim. 4:2), but he must also encourage and comfort. It is doubtful that anyone but a pastor knows how difficult it is to preach to the same group of people twice every Sunday and make a talk at prayer meeting every Wednesday night. There must always be something new and fresh and worth-while to say. The pastor of the small church also must plan for all of the organizations and perform a thousand and one tasks that in a larger church are done by others. It is more than any man can do in his own strength and wisdom.

A praying church can make a great pastor and a great preacher out of very ordinary material. Great preachers and pastors, such as Spurgeon, have faithful groups of praying Christians by their sides. Happy is the pastor of whom it can be said as it was said of Saul, when he was chosen to be Israel's first king, "There went with him a band of men, whose hearts God had touched" (1 Sam. 10:26). A cold and prayerless church is usually an unsympathetic, demanding, and critical church that can break a pastor's heart. The pastor of a large city church of my own denomination, a man with the soul of a poet and seer, was bearing an intolerable burden of opposition by an active, insidious, determined, and conscienceless minority. When he fell fainting in his pulpit one Sunday evening, his son sprang to his father's aid and cried to the startled congregation, "You have finally killed him!" I fear that the accusation was sadly and literally true, although the pastor survived that attack.

One day an elderly maiden lady in a church where I had been pastor only a few months said to me with quiet dignity, "Most of the members of my missionary circle have covenanted together to pray for you each day, and we have done so for the past three months. I thought you would like to know it."

I replied honestly: "I did not know what it was, but for the past three months I have felt a new spirit of confidence and power. It has been easy to prepare my sermons, and I feel an ease and freedom in the pulpit that I had not known. I know one of the reasons now, and I thank you for telling me. I hope you keep it up."

We should pray for Sunday school teachers, for church officers, for the leaders of the young people, for the choir. Here is a ministry every member of the church who is a Christian can perform. It may be that your circumstances or talents are not such that you have been called to teach, or lead, or sing in the choir; but you can share in the work by your prayers.

We should pray for our missionaries. Hallesby has told of a missionary who was about to sail for a mission post in a place where the tropical fevers had undermined the health of many missionaries. Those who did not die had to leave after a few years of service. As he went around in his home community to tell his friends good-by, he came upon an elderly believing woman in a tenant household. She clung to his hand and, looking him calmly in the eye, said quietly but with great sincerity: "I am going to pray to God for you and ask him to save you from the fever in order that you may devote all your strength to your work out there."

Afterwards, the missionary told of this experience with deep emotion: "And I have not felt the fever once during all these years!" [2]

We should pray for one another. Those who are yet "babes in Christ" need our prayers that they may grow in grace and in the knowledge of Jesus Christ. We should pray for those who are subject to strong temptations, "considering thyself, lest thou also be tempted" (Gal. 6:1). We should pray for those who have heavy burdens to bear—poverty, sickness, sorrow, and other kinds of trouble. Thus we may help bear each other's burdens. We should pray for those who have a spirit of

---

[2] *Ibid.*, p. 72.

worldliness or indifference, that they may be led to a closer walk with God.

But just here a word of caution needs to be spoken. The spirit in which we undertake a ministry of intercession is of utmost importance. Sometimes the statement, "I am praying for you," may be made in such a manner as to arouse resentment, so as to be almost an insult. Thus a person may say, by his attitude, "You need my prayers, and in spite of your faults, I am big enough to pray for you." One of the greatest foes of the spiritual life is the sin of spiritual pride—the sin of the Pharisee. Even the high priest in Old Testament times, when he was about to make a sin-offering for the people, was required first to make an atonement for his own sins. That was necessary both as a preventive of spiritual pride and self-righteousness, and because he also was a sinner, and he could not come into the holy of holies until his hands were clean and his heart was right.

Whenever we feel the least tendency to pharisaism, we ought to stop praying for others and pray only for ourselves until we recognize *our* need of the prayers of the humblest Christian in our behalf. Nor can we substitute prayer for others for our personal obedience to the call of duty. If we ought to be working at a task to which God has called us, no amount of prayer for others will excuse us. When I knew that the Lord had called me to be a preacher, when I wanted to study law, I tried to make a deal with the Lord. If he would let me be a lawyer, I would be a very faithful church member, do anything my pastor wanted me to do as a layman, and support the church with the large sums of money I expected to make practicing law. It didn't work.

Nor are we excused from the ministry of intercession because we are working at Kingdom tasks. A number of years ago I covenanted to pray for a former schoolmate who was doing evangelistic work. In the multitude of tasks as a busy pastor, husband, and father I often forgot. One day I was in my study trying to prepare a sermon, when something reminded me of my covenant. I tried to put it out of my mind and to concentrate upon the sermon. But a voice within persisted: "Pray for H—— A—— *now*." I knelt in front of my desk. Immediately a heavy and anxious burden for my friend lay upon my shoulders, and I prayed earnestly and desperately for the Lord to empower and guide my friend wherever he was. I prayed until the burden was eased, and I felt that a victory had been won. I do not understand it yet, and make no effort to explain it.

Our own part of the work of the kingdom should never become too great for us to remember our comrades in service, and to pray for them. Jesus often prayed that his followers be one, as he and the Father are one. I know of nothing that will more quickly and surely unite Christians in real worldwide fellowship than intercessory prayer for all the household of faith, for all kingdom interests, and for all the workers of the kingdom.

IX

Ineffective Prayer

And then, when you pray, don't be like the play-actors.
They love to stand and pray in the synagogues and at street-
corners so that people may see them at it. Believe me, they
have had all the reward they are going to get. . . . And
when you pray don't rattle off long prayers like the pagans
who think they will be heard because they use a lot of
words. Don't be like them. After all God, Who is your Father, knows your needs before you ask Him.

MATTHEW 6:5–8, PHILLIPS

Two kinds of "prayer" Jesus condemned as ineffective
in this passage from the Sermon on the Mount. One
is prayer that is mere play-acting, designed to impress
men with a sense of one's piety. The other is prayer that
reflects a pagan conception of God, as a potentate to be
impressed with noise and the endless repetition of
words, rather than the compassionate Heavenly Father
who knows the needs of his children and is always at-
tentive to their simple requests. Jesus' parable of the
Pharisee and the publican illustrates the futility of
prayer by the proud, the kind of prayer that is no more
than communing with oneself in self-congratulation.

Since prayer is for the Christian—as Hallesby put it—
"nothing more involved than to let Jesus into our needs,"
the examples cited here are not prayer at all, in the
Christian sense. Nevertheless, such "praying" is practiced by some Christians and deserves our critical exami-
nation. Of course we realize that certain other approaches to prayer are ineffective: prayer that does not
put first the kingdom of God and his righteousness,

prayer from a disobedient and rebellious heart, prayer
without faith, utterly selfish prayer.

To all honest men there is something obnoxious about
the thoroughgoing hypocrite. This is a little strange
since people expect and like a certain amount of hypocrisy. People like to be "made over," even when they
know that the effusive greeting and flattery doesn't
really mean anything. Successful politicians make every
man feel that he is important; they will listen to every
man's views, however weird, and laugh at his jokes, no
matter how stale. People know that they are playing a
part, but they still get the vote. Men's suits are padded
at the shoulders to give the wearer a more robust appearance, and women choose clothing that will accen-
tuate their slimness, especially if they are inclined the
other way. These harmless little hypocrisies are part of
accepted custom and good manners.

But the person who is *always* acting a part, pretend-
ing emotions that he does not feel, speaking unctuous
words that he does not mean, professing a loyalty that
does not exist, and exuding a studied charm that can be
turned on and off like an electric light, becomes a thor-
ough hypocrite. His whole life is a lie, and unless res-
cued by divine grace, he reaches the point where he
himself cannot discern between his true convictions and
the mask of claims that he makes for personal advantage. Such a person never sees himself in a mirror, but
sees instead the person he imagines himself to be. Of all
sinners the hypocrite received the condemnation of
Jesus, who loved all real men—even sinners.

One cannot imagine a more despicable and dangerous
pretense than a hypocritical prayer. In Jesus' day certain hours were set for prayer, and the Pharisees whom
Jesus described took pains to be at some busy street

corner when those hours arrived so that they could stop in full sight of the crowd and pray. They wanted men to see and hear them, to admire their piety, devotion, and eloquence. When Jesus taught his disciples, he chose his words well: "When thou prayest"—not when the hour of prayer has arrived, but rather when the heart moves one to pray. It was not the place or posture that Jesus condemned; one may pray standing or walking, and at any place. He scored the motive: "to be seen of men." The Pharisees expected that men should observe their pious practice. That is what they wanted, and that is *all* that they could get—that, and nothing else. "They *have* their reward."

Many people through the ages have been disturbed by this passage, wondering whether it forbids all public prayer and group praying. Theophylact, who lived in the eleventh century, asks: "What then? Shall I not pray in church? By all means, *but with a right intention,* and without display, for it is not the place that hurts, but the manner and the aim." Chrysostom said: "Some, even when their person is concealed, make themselves manifest to all by their voice." [1]

A lady in a town where I was pastor once complained about a preacher of one of the emotional sects. He lived about a block away and frequently awakened the whole neighborhood at two or three o'clock in the morning with the "fervency" of his praying. Of course it is commendable for a preacher to pray earnestly at any hour of the night, but it is not necessary for him to awaken his neighbors in order to gain the ear of God.

Undoubtedly, the Model Prayer is designed for group praying, for the personal pronoun throughout is plural:

---

[1] John A. Broadus, *Commentary on Matthew* (Philadelphia: American Baptist Publication Society, 1886), p. 140.

"Our Father . . . Give us . . . And forgive us." The disciples were praying as a group in the upper room when the fire fell and the Power came at Pentecost. It was not their praying but the answer to their prayer that was "noised abroad." The church was praying when the "second Pentecost" came, as recorded in the fourth chapter of Acts. There are many examples and accounts of congregational praying in the New Testament. Public prayer has its place—a very vital place—in the life and work of the church. But here, as elsewhere, the motive and intention must be right.

I was once praying with a friend about a mutual problem on which we were not agreed. When I had finished, the other said quietly: "To whom was that prayer addressed?" Then I realized that unconsciously I had been arguing my side of the problem in the prayer. I had not really wanted God to show us the way out of our dilemma. Instead, I tried to change my friend's mind. In short, I was praying for the ears of a man rather than God. True prayer is communion with God, and is a heart-searching business.

Jesus also condemned "heathen" praying in these words: "Use not vain repetitions, as the heathen do." "Empty phrases" and "idle rote" are other translations. They expect to be heard "for their much speaking" or "their many words." Immediately, we recall the experience of Elijah on Mount Carmel when the priests of Baal cried from early morning until noon: "Baal, hear us!" They leaped upon the altar, shouting and cutting themselves with stones, until Elijah sarcastically suggested that perhaps their "god" was asleep or had gone on a journey! Buddhist monks will for whole days cry aloud in monotonous repetition the sacred syllable "Um!" Again, Broadus claims that "after a Mohammedan funeral in some countries, devout men assemble, and repeat Allah el Allah three thousand times." [2] If this is heathen practice, what about repeating "Hail, Mary," or "Pater Noster" from fifteen to fifty times, keeping count by passing beads through the fingers? (Incidentally, the use of the rosary is of Buddhist origin, was later adopted by the Mohammedans, and by them carried into Spain, where it passed into "Christian" usage, and from the Spanish Catholics down to our generation.)

Or what shall we say to an "orgy or prayer," in which an entire congregation prays aloud at the same time— each his own prayer—until the sound is bedlam? Or what of prayers through which run a chant of a few phrases repeated so rapidly that the "worshiper" loses control of his tongue and intellect and utters unintelligible jargon? What of prayer practices that are intended to storm the ramparts of heaven with such a deluge of words, with such a furor of sound, that the gates will be battered down and God compelled reluctantly to hear? Is God deaf that he cannot hear? Is he asleep that he must be awakened by our noise? Is he to be moved with the frenzy of words or convinced by eloquent argument? "Your Father knoweth what things ye have need of, before you ask him," said Jesus. But he wants us to ask reverently, earnestly, with faith, and with the patient persistence that faith inspires. It is not eloquence but earnestness, not sound but sincerity, not frenzy but faith, that God desires in prayer.

Pride makes prayer ineffective. In the parable of the Pharisee and the publican, we should notice that it is not the place or posture that makes the difference. Both

---

[2] *Ibid.*, p. 130.

men were in the Temple, both were standing as they prayed, but there the similarity ended. "The Pharisee stood and prayed thus *with himself*, God, I thank thee, that I am not as other men are, extortioners, unjust, adulterers, or even as this publican. I fast twice in the week, I give tithes of all that I possess."

"Prayed thus with himself!" Is there such satire as this in all literature? He did *address* God, but he was really indulging in self-adulation. Like "little Jack Horner" he was saying: "What a good boy am I!" He did not recognize the holiness of God that causes all men to see their own sinfulness. He did not appreciate God's mercy and grace that could enable a man to escape the tragedy of bearing the image of God marred and perverted by his human heritage. This man was his own god. Prayer for him was communion with his own ego.

The publican, on the other hand, standing perhaps in a shadowy corner, bowed his head in the "house of prayer." Then, aware of the presence of God, filled with the sense of his need, in a sudden involuntary expression of his guilt, beat his breast, and cried out, "God be merciful to me, a sinner!"

Jesus was pointed in his evaluation of the prayer approaches of the strictly righteous Pharisee and the despised publican. "I tell you, this man went down to his house justified rather than the other: for every one that exalteth himself shall be abased; and he that humbleth himself shall be exalted."

X

Praying in Secret

But thou, when thou prayest, enter into thine inner chamber, and having shut thy door, pray to thy Father who is in secret, and thy Father who seeth in secret shall recompense thee.

MATTHEW 6:6, ASV

Over against the pretentious prayers of the hypocritical Pharisee, Jesus taught his followers, when they prayed, to go into their room, shut the door, and make prayer a communion with God alone.

What then was the meaning of Daniel's practice when he defied the king's decree? He opened his window, turned his face toward Jerusalem, and prayed for all the world to see his confidence in Jehovah. He could have prayed secretly, but Daniel had a witness to bear. The people were watching to see if Daniel would alter his prayer habits through fear of the king.

Of course, the king's decree was a foolish one, for no man can prevent another from praying to his God. He may cast him into a dark dungeon with neither candle nor prayer book, but prayers from a dungeon are heard as readily as prayers offered in the Temple. He may put a gag in a man's mouth and bind him hand and foot, but prayers do not depend upon spoken words.

Jesus did not condemn public prayer in its place, but he did emphasize the power of secret prayer. Dr. Dixon once said: "Prayer may be public or private, but it must always be secret in the sense that it is a personal transaction between the soul and God. Even if one thousand people should join in the same prayer, only those would

really pray who deal personally with God." [1] Which is
another way of saying that prayer must be a sincere effort for the heart, soul, and mind of man to commune
with God. Dr. R. G. Lee says: "We need to get into the
private place *with* God before we go into the public
place *for* God. We need to be in the closet *with* God before we go into the conflict *for* God and for others. We
need to *hide* ourselves with God before we *show* ourselves for God." [2]

Why did Jesus recommend the closed room? To shut
out the distractions of the world perhaps. But the world
can invade even the privacy of a closed room. But if
shutting the door, is an expression of true desire to be
alone with God, it gives impetus to the prayer purpose.
In the closed room we can pray aloud without embarrassment, and without any thought of the impression
our words make upon others. We are alone with God.
We may strip ourselves of all pretense, discard any out-
ward show of righteousness, drop our shield of self-
confidence, and without restraint bring our deep need,
our fears, our ignorance, our uncertainty into the very
presence of the God "which seeth in secret." In the
closed room no one can pretend a faith that he does not
possess, or a confidence that he does not feel. Only
God is there to see and hear, and we may wait there in
an agony of spirit until we feel his presence.

The closed room becomes, first of all, a *confessional*—
a deep need in every life. The Roman Catholic Church
recognizes that need, and requires its members to confess to the priest who assumes God's prerogative to forgive sins or to assess acts of penance as a means to

[1] Quoted by R. G. Lee, *The Bible and Prayer* (Nashville: Broadman Press, 1950), p. 48.
[2] *Ibid.*, pp. 47–48.

forgiveness. There is no doubt but that the penitent experiences a sense of relief when he turns the problem of his sin over to the Church. The psychologist helps relieve mental tensions by leading his patient to "unload" his burdened soul. Every pastor becomes at times a confessor, whether he wants to be or not. If he is wise, he leads the person who is weighed down with a sense of guilt to confess his sins unto God, and to seek his forgiveness. "If we confess our sins, he is faithful and just to forgive us our sins, and to cleanse us from all unrighteousness" (1 John 1:9).

But there is no need of an intermediary between man and God save "the man Christ Jesus," who has become our High Priest forever. In the secret place with God the closed room becomes a holy place, with both altar and mercy seat. There we may lay bare our very souls and unburden our hearts to our Heavenly Father. Struggling to put our guilt into words, we are aware that "we know not what we should pray for as we ought," and we remember that "the Spirit itself maketh intercession for us with groanings which cannot be uttered" (Rom. 8:26). Once we have opened the gates of pride, our confession pours forth as a mountain stream breaking through the ice and slush of winter.

The closed room is also a *place of vision.*

All of us have dreams and aspirations, often vague and nebulous, which we would hesitate to confess to another person, lest he prove void of understanding or unsympathetic. Yet the need of sharing with *Someone* these treasures of the inner self becomes imperative if the dormant forces that produced them are expressed rather than repressed. Sometimes we do not understand the urges and drives that possess us, but we can talk to God about them, remembering that he "giveth to all

men liberally, and upbraideth not." Isaiah was alone
with his depression and aspirations when he "saw also
the Lord, high and lifted up," and heard his call:
"Whom shall I send, and who will go for us?" It was
just what he needed, and he answered: "Here am I;
send me" (Isa. 6:8). Almost too sacred to relate are
three experiences of my own, but I tell them to illustrate
what I am trying to say.

The first occurred when I was about fifteen or sixteen.
Near the country church we attended was a ridge of
huge boulders. In one place they formed a sort of a
natural chamber with sandy floor, shut in on all sides
but open towards heaven. On a Sunday afternoon during the summer revival I went there strangely disturbed.
I had already been saved, and I could not understand
the cause of my restless and unhappy spirit. As I tried
to pray, the conviction was borne in upon me that the
Lord wanted me to preach his Word. I had secretly believed that some day the Lord would call me to preach,
but I had thought the "call" would be an audible voice
or some other supernatural demonstration. Instead, it
was a simple conviction born in the heart. Aware of my
unworthiness and inability, I stood in awe before the
knowledge that in this alone I should find peace of mind
and a meaning to life. As much as I was then able, I
promised God that I would follow where he led. Would
to God that I had followed that vision from that hour
without wavering!

Years later on board a transport returning from
France at the close of World War I, the same boy, suddenly become a man by the alchemy of war, I left the
stuffy quarters below deck and sought sanctuary on the
deck at midnight. I had to pray. I finally found a place
somewhat sheltered from the wind and spray. The Feb-
ruary night was stormy, and the huge ship was tossed

by the waves like a piece of flotsam. Not a person was in sight, except the dim figure of the watch high on the officers' deck. I felt alone with God in the middle of the stormy ocean—and I was not afraid. I meditated upon the providence of God that had brought me unscathed through the war. What would I do with my life, now that I would soon be home, and a civilian again? The memory of the experience in the rocks had never left me, and now it returned with a deep poignancy. I thanked God for his mercies, and promised that I *would* preach his Word.

But before I got home, I had secured a job traveling for a great newspaper. I took it with the idea of accumulating some money in order that I might go to school to prepare myself for the task. Soon, busily immersed in the work, I began to dream of a career as a journalist when I had served my apprenticeship. But I was not happy. My weekly salary seemed to run through my fingers unnoticed. By midsummer I was in a hotel room in a north Texas city for the week end. I could not sleep. About midnight I fell upon my knees by the side of my bed and sought the throne of grace. It was not easy, for a Voice seemed to ring in my heart: "Preacher, the time is *now!*" I was even less fit for the task than when I first became conscious of the call, but I found no peace until I made the complete surrender.

Monday morning I called my employer and resigned. I went home, and on Wednesday night I told the church of my call, my long struggle against it, and my surrender. I was granted a license that night, and have never turned back. Only one of these experiences occurred in a room with a closed door, but in each of them I was in a *secret place* with God.

The closed room is often the *gateway to fellowship with God.* "He that dwelleth in the secret place of the most High shall abide under the shadow of the Almighty." In this busy, practical, prosaic age we hear little about the "secret of His presence," about the blessedness of fellowship of the saints with their God. When it is mentioned, the multitudes do not understand. God, to them, is an idea which one accepts as being the most agreeable explanation of life, a comfortable philosophy. They like to hear about God's power and wisdom, his redeeming love, and his everlasting mercy. Many would like to know more about how to *get* things from God, but the hunger for the divine Companion as a need of the soul seems to be a rare thing. The hunger is there, the need is there, and our lives are poor until it is satisfied, but we often do not recognize it.

Now and then some rare mystic or some ordinary man, driven by circumstance, discovers the fact that men can know God in intimate, personal fellowship, and he *shows* us that it is true. Admiral Richard E. Byrd, in his book of 1938 entitled *Alone*, tells of his terrible experience in an advanced outpost for many weary months alone. One night when he could not sleep, he wrote in his diary: "The human race, then, is not alone in the universe. Though I am cut off from human beings, *I* am not alone."

John G. Magee, son of American missionaries to China, joined the Canadian Air Force during World War II and became a test pilot. At the age of nineteen he fell to his death in an airplane. But he left these lines about his spiritual adventure while flying at an altitude of 30,000 feet above England:

Oh! I have slipped the surly bonds of earth
    And danced the skies on laughter-silvered wings;
Sunward I've climbed, and joined the tumbling mirth
    Of sun-split clouds—and done a hundred things

You have not dreamed of—wheeled and soared and swung
   High in the sunlit silence. Hovering there,
I've chased the shouting wind along, and flung
   My eager craft through footless halls of air.

Up, up the long delirious, burning blue
   I've topped the wind-swept heights with easy grace
Where never lark, or even eagle flew—
   And, while with silent lifting mind I've trod
The high untrespassed sanctity of space,
   Put out my hand and touched the face of God.[3]

These men were both terribly alone when they found
fellowship with God, and we may find it in the closed
room in secret prayer.

Finally, the closed room is a *place of power*.

Cleansing, vision, fellowship—then power. Power for
self-mastery; power to follow the gleam; power over
circumstance, since our fellowship is with him who
walks with us in all of life's way; and power for the
tasks that are ours. In Greek mythology we find the
story of a fight between Hercules and a giant who was
the son of Mother Earth. Whenever Hercules threw the
giant to the ground, his mother renewed his strength,
and he arose refreshed. Hercules was able to defeat
him only by lifting him clear of the earth, separating
him from the source of his power. Only when Satan is
able to keep us out of the secret place of prayer is he
able to have his way with us, or defeat us.

Enter into thine inner chamber, and having shut thy
door, pray to thy Father who is in secret, and thy Father
who seeth in secret shall recompense thee.

---

[3] "Sunward I've Climbed" in *Masterpieces of Religious Verse*,
Morrison, *op. cit.*, used by permission.

XI

Moving Mountains

"If you had faith as a grain of mustard seed, you could say to this sycamine tree, 'Be rooted up, and be planted in the sea,' and it would obey you." Luke 17:5–6, RSV

"Have faith in God. Truly, I say to you, whoever says to this mountain, 'Be taken up and cast into the sea,' and *does not doubt in his heart,* but believes that what he says will come to pass, it will be done for him. Therefore I tell you, whatever you ask in prayer, *believe that you receive it,* and you will." Mark 11:22–24, RSV

"Why could not we cast it out?" He said to them, "Because of your little faith. For truly, I say to you, *if you have faith* as a grain of mustard seed, you will say to this mountain, 'Move hence to yonder place,' and it will move; and *nothing will be impossible to you."* Matthew 17:19–20, RSV

Only one of these passages appears, at first glance, to refer to prayer. The others seem to deal primarily with supernatural power possessed by the man who has faith. The passage in Mark 11 relates this to prayer. The man who has faith can command *things* to obey him, and can *receive* from God what he asks in faith.

One unfailing rule for correct interpretation of Scripture is to discover first just what was said and the occasion upon which it was said. Let us see first what Jesus said in each instance and the circumstance in which he spoke. In opening verses of Luke 17 he said:

"Temptations to sin are sure to come; but woe to him by whom they come! It would be better for him if a millstone were hung round his neck and he were cast into the sea, than that he should cause one of these little ones to sin."

Then, without a break, he went on:

"Take heed to yourselves; if your brother sins, rebuke him, and if he repents, forgive him; and if he sins against you seven times in the day, and turns to you seven times, and says, 'I repent,' you must forgive him."

It was a double dose. "How in the world," the disciples must have thought, "can we be sure that no action, word, or attitude of ours shall cause a weaker brother, or young person, to be tempted to sin? How can we have the patience and forbearance to keep on forgiving a fellow who 'gets in our hair' seven times in one day? 'This is a hard saying, who can bear it.' *Increase our faith.*"

In Mark 11 and Matthew 21, the disciples asked why the barren fig tree upon which Jesus had pronounced a curse because it had nothing but leaves should be withered to the ground. It was to them, as I must confess it is to me, an inexplicable mystery. And we come upon them every day and ask ourselves, "Why? How?" For instance, a man seemingly in the midst of virile manhood, head of a fine family, a pillar in the church, a useful and needed man in the community, whose influence for good is felt by all who know him, is suddenly stricken by disease and dies. His family, the church, the community need him. But a drunken neighbor—no good to his family, the church, or the community—lives on to old age. If one man had to die, why not he? The answer? "Have faith in God." Sometimes that is the only answer we can give.

In Matthew 17 the disciples had failed to cast out the evil spirit from the afflicted boy. When Jesus came, the distressed father turned to him. " 'If you can do anything, have pity on us, and help us.' And Jesus said to him, 'If you can! All things are possible to him who believes' " (Mark 9:22–23, RSV). Later the disciples asked, " 'Why could we not cast it out?' " Some translations differ on Jesus' answer: "Because of your *no faith*" or "your little faith." I incline to the former reading, because Jesus said: " 'If you have faith *as a grain of mustard seed.*' " In relation to the problem they had *no* faith in their power to heal the lad.

Bringing all the problems together, the disciples were asking: How can we live in the world as Christians are supposed to live so that both our deeds and our *influence* shall be righteous? How can we achieve such unselfish love that we shall be able to forgive our brother as often as we need God's forgiveness? How can we learn to accept life's inexplicable mysteries? How can we do the work that God has given us to do?

Jesus' answer is quite plain: Have faith in God. Rid your hearts of all doubt. When you ask anything in prayer, believe that you receive.

But the answer goes far beyond the particular problems that aroused the questions. With this sort of faith what you command will happen; what you ask will be yours; nothing shall be impossible to you.

Let it be admitted at once that these Scripture passages present a problem that is not easily resolved. Here we leave the kindergarten of prayer to enrol for a postgraduate course. When I first began preaching the series of sermons on the teachings of Jesus concerning prayer out of which this book grew, I had trouble with this one. After working on it for weeks, I laid it aside, and went on with the others. Then something happened.

Shortly after I moved to my present pastorate, I

began to be troubled with hoarseness that had no discoverable cause. I did not have a cold, and there was no soreness in the throat. Facing a revival in the near future in which I was to do the preaching, I went to a throat specialist. He discovered a small nodule on my vocal chord and commanded me not to use my voice at all. In spite of my protests he gave me a pad of paper and told me to *write* whatever I had to say to anyone. He even called my wife in and told her that I must not even whisper. I was able to get a preacher for the meeting, and I attended, shook hands with the people, and smiled. At the close of the meeting, I went back to the doctor, and he reported that the growth was diminishing. My wife asked him how long I would have to remain silent. His reply *floored* me. "Probably six months!"

Next morning I was in the hospital for an exploratory operation. To his surprise and my consternation, the growth was malignant. The vocal chord could be removed, and I could spend the rest of my life croaking, or we could use the mysterious rays that God had put in the universe, that Roentgen had discovered, and probably save my voice. Of course, I had already prayed about the matter. I could not believe that it was the will of God that a little cancer no larger than a pinhead should end my career as a preacher.

I turned my case over to God and to the doctors. There was no lack of faith in asking the doctors to use the rays God had created, and the skill God had given them, any more than we show a lack of faith in God's power to sustain life when we eat food. For six weeks my throat was exposed daily to this invisible energy that can destroy as well as cure. I am grateful to God that never once, during this long ordeal, was there the least shadow of a doubt that the "mountain" should be

removed. On the contrary, I found occasion to thank
God for the experience. The noble way in which the
membership of my church rallied to the aid of their
pastor strengthened our bonds of fellowship. The first
sermon I preached on returning to my pulpit was:
"Moving Mountains."

What shall we do with these words of Jesus?

We may, of course, ignore them and pass on to something easier to understand. Many people do this, some
of them Christian leaders—even some who write books
on prayer. We may explain them away to our own satis-
faction. Some, without fully realizing what they are
doing, accept the deadly heresy that many of the teachings of Jesus reflect the superstitions of his day. What
they are really saying is that Jesus was only a man. But
to those who believe with John that Jesus Christ is the
divine Logos, who was "in the beginning with God,"
who himself created all things, and who "became flesh,
and dwelt among us"; who believe him when he said:
"I am the way, the truth, and the life," and who believe
with Paul that "in him dwelleth all the fulness of the
Godhead bodily"—to them *every word of Jesus is true*.
Any other attitude is a deadly heresy. Unless Jesus *knew*
what he was talking about, unless every word spoken
by him concerning God, man, life, and eternity is true,
we cannot risk our immortal souls on any of them.

The trouble with my generation is that we have witnessed so many triumphs of science in discovering the
secrets of the universe that we believed that science is
the only method of ascertaining truth. Science that gave
us radio, automobiles, television, jet planes, radar, and
a thousand and one things to transform our ways of
living and thinking became the god we worshiped, the
new "messiah" that should usher in the millennium. The

axioms of science became our decalogue, its laws our moral code, and its techniques "the way, the truth, and the life."

But the generation now assuming leadership should be able to see that science and its machines, uncontrolled by some higher Power, may not only rob us of the freedom to live any decent sort of life, but may destroy both our civilization and the race. Science is a jealous god and cannot endure a rival. But when we regard science as a God-given servant to help man subdue the world, as God commanded Adam; and when we remember that the God who created the universe is not limited by that which he created, we can believe again in what we call "miracles," for lack of a better term. It has always seemed strange to me that men, performing quite nonchalantly some feats that our fathers would have called miracles, and our grandfathers witchcraft, should doubt *any*thing. *We* are able to perform "miracles" because we have discovered and learned to use powers that always existed. How do we know that God, who created it all, does not have powers that we have not yet discovered?

Of course, we can make these words of Jesus sound quite ridiculous by interpreting them to mean that men with faith are given unlimited powers unconditionally. In his fascinating story "The Man Who Could Work Miracles" H. G. Wells tells of a man who suddenly received power that enabled him to command anything to happen and it happened. It was fun for a while. Although he did not use his power maliciously or selfishly, he presently got things in such a mess that his last command was that everything be put back just like it was when he started running the universe. Then the man prayed that the power be taken from him. Of course things *would* get confused—because he was mortal.

A review of a recent book on prayer presented the following hypothetical problem: A man is making a journey along an unpaved road in an automobile, and he prays that he may have fair weather for his journey. But at the same time a group of farmers who live beside that same road pray for rain upon their parched fields. Both the traveler and the farmers have faith in God's promise to answer prayer. The writer asks: "What is God to do?"

Certainly, Jesus did not mean to teach that men were to be given such unlimited and unconditional power that God would be in a quandary as to which prayer of faith he would answer.

Nor did Jesus expect his words to be accepted with such literalness that men should go about moving a mountain from one place to another, or uprooting trees and setting them out in the sea. What in the world would be the use of that? That would be as foolish as the actions of the cult that accepts literally the doubtful words added to Mark's Gospel, brings live snakes to church, and torments them into biting.

What *did* Jesus mean? We must remember that "no prophecy of the scripture is of any private interpretation." That is, we cannot lift one passage out of the Word and treat it as a separate and independent truth. We must interpret every Scripture passage in relation to all other Scripture. In our study of the teachings of Jesus on prayer we have noticed that in prayer:

Children are addressing their heavenly Father.

Worshipers are adoring their God, whose name is hallowed.

Subjects are acknowledging that the kingdom of God is their supreme concern.

Humbly and obediently they pray that God's will be done.

"If ye shall ask any thing *in my name,* I will do it" (John 14:14).

"If ye abide in me, and my words abide in you, ye shall ask what ye will" (John 15:7).

What we ask, therefore, as children of God must consider the interests of the kingdom of God, must be in accordance with his will, must be asked in the name of Jesus by those who *abide* in him, and in whom his words abide. Surely, with these limitations, we cannot ask foolishly, or maliciously, or selfishly, "in faith, nothing doubting."

I believe that Jesus intended in these passages to teach, dramatically and strikingly, the truth he was always endeavoring to get his followers to grasp—the omnipotence of God. When he said it was easier for a camel to go through the eye of a needle than for a rich man to enter the kingdom of heaven, the disciples asked: "Who then can be saved?" Jesus answered: "With men this is impossible; but with God all things are possible." "Faith as a grain of mustard seed"—against yon mountain—the smallest thing imaginable against the biggest thing in sight! It was a truth they needed, that little band of ordinary men, given a gleam of the Eternal, presently to be left alone to face a hostile and unbelieving world with a message that challenged all that they lived by. They needed to know that unlimited power, perfect wisdom, and assured victory could be theirs through faith. It is the assurance that we need today, as we quake in our boots or whistle in the glare of the atom bomb and the H-bomb, or at the sound of guided missiles and supersonic jets—*manned by our enemies.* It is the assurance we need today as we see

our children mingling with a society that seems to be
on its way to paganism in so many respects.

Surely, we have already discovered anew that we cannot build the kingdom of God—or even its counterfeit,
utopia—by our own wisdom and in our own strength.
We need the *faith that moves mountains!*

What is this faith?

The Bible has only one *definition* of faith, in Hebrews 11:1. "Now faith is the *assurance* of things hoped
for, the conviction of things not seen." The Greek word
translated "assurance" or "substance," as in the King
James Version, is *hupostasis*, literally, something standing under, as the foundation of a house.

With that definition in mind, we see new meaning in
Jesus' words: "Whatever you ask in prayer, *believe that
you receive it*, and you will." That is faith giving substance to the things asked for in prayer, *before* it is
actually in hand.

Moses "endured [in his choice], as seeing him who
is invisible." What absurdity is this—seeing that which
cannot be seen! But that is the realm in which faith
works. Remember Elisha and his servant at Dothan.
Elisha prayed that the Lord would "open the eyes" of
his frightened servant that he might see the circling
mountains filled with the chariots of God and know that
"they that be with us are more than they that be with
them." Again, when Peter drew his sword to defend his
Lord against the band that came to arrest him, Jesus
said: "Thinkest thou that I cannot now pray to my
Father, and he shall presently give me more than twelve
legions of angels?" (Matt. 26:53). He did not ask for
them, and they were invisible, but Jesus knew they were
there and available.

With similar faith the aged apostle John wrote: "Beloved, if our hearts condemn us not, then have we confidence toward God. And whatsoever we ask, we receive of him, because we keep his commandments, and do those things that are pleasing in his sight." We need never fear again. Nothing can happen to us that is not within the will of God. If it is his will, it is best for us. There are no insurmountable difficulties, no impossible tasks, when we have faith in God. "This is the victory" John concluded, "that overcometh the world, even our faith."

XII

The Persistence of Faith

> He told them a parable, to the effect that they ought always to pray and not lose heart.
>
> LUKE 18:1, RSV

Jesus told the parable in Luke 18:1–8 to teach that "men ought always to pray, and not to faint" or "lose heart." It is usually called the parable of the unjust judge; therefore, many commentators say that it does not teach importunity in prayer, since God is not like the unjust judge. But it is better called the parable of the persistent widow, or the "importunate widow." Certainly she is the moving character in the story. The judge, who "neither feared God nor regarded man," ignored the widow's plea until she wearied him so with her continual coming that he acted only in order to get rid of her.

The widow knew that the judge had the authority to vindicate her, and she believed so strongly in the justice of her case that she was confident that even the proud judge would finally heed her plea. Then Jesus "applied" the parable: "Will not God vindicate his elect, *who* cry to him day and night? Will he delay long over them? I tell you, he will vindicate them speedily. Nevertheless, when the Son of man comes, will he find faith on earth?"

The same lesson is taught, and so stated, in the parable of the embarrassed host in Luke 11:5–8. It does not illustrate the nature of God, for the ungracious neighbor does not represent God any more than does the unjust judge. Embarrassed by his inability to set food before his unexpected guest, the host finally persevered with his ungracious neighbor "because of his importunity." Jesus then added: "Ask, and it shall be given you; seek, and ye shall find; knock, and it shall be opened unto you." If the mere asking always received an immediate answer, seeking and knocking would seem superfluous. Two things would seem to be essential to the "effectual fervent prayer" that "availeth much": Our need must be genuine, earnest, and just, and we must have the faith in God's power and goodness to persevere until we know that we have an answer. It may finally be "No," but by that time we will see that what we thought we wanted was not really best for us. In fact, the answer may be something far better than we asked.

Two strange incidents in the earthly life of our Lord do not seem at first to reflect at all the nature and spirit of Jesus.

The first involved Mary and Martha and their brother, Lazarus. You recall that these three were intimate friends of Jesus, and that he often enjoyed their hospitality in the quiet little suburb of Bethany. John reminds us that it was Mary who anointed Jesus with costly ointment, washed his feet with her tears, and dried them with her hair. One day an urgent message came to Jesus: "He whom thou lovest is sick." How strangely did he comment on this news!

" 'This illness is not unto death; it is for the glory of God, so that the Son of God may be glorified by the means of it.' So when he heard that he was ill, *he stayed two days longer in the place where he was*" (John 11:4, 6, RSV).

But Mary and Martha did not know this. They had sent an urgent message to One who was able to heal all manner of disease with a word or a touch, and they must have watched anxiously the road by which he would come while Lazarus grew steadily worse. Perhaps the sick man called for his friend. Finally he died. And no word had come from Jesus.

Shocked and heartsick, Mary and Martha watched the neighbors prepare the body for burial, and received expressions of sympathy and condolence from their friends. The tomb was opened, and the body, wrapped in grave clothes and spices, was buried.

Still Jesus did not come.

Four days after the funeral, Jesus came. Martha went out to meet him. Why did not Mary go? She was the one who sat at the feet of Jesus while Martha busied herself about the household tasks, providing for the comfort of their Guest. It was Mary whose extravagant act of love elicited the ever-to-be-remembered appreciation of Jesus. One can only imagine the tragic undertones, the desperate searching of the heart for an explanation of the strange delay, in Martha's words of greeting: "Lord, if you had been here, my brother would not have died." Or the hopeful faith as she continued: "And even now I know that whatever you ask from God, God will give you." It was Martha's faith that persevered unto death, and beyond!

Jesus' answer to this paean of persistent faith has brought comfort and hope to bereaved hearts through the centuries. Dr. Joseph Fort Newton in *River of Years*, tells of his boyhood impressions of his father's funeral in a rural community in northeast Texas. It was a cold, blustery day, and the whole earth seemed wrapped in a gray sort of darkness through which the snow was falling. He said: "The old country minister adjusted his glasses and read the words of Jesus, 'I am the resurrection and the life—Let not your hearts be troubled.' Never shall I forget the power of those words. It was as if a great, gentle Hand, stronger than the hand of man and more tender than the hand of any woman, had been put forth from the Unseen to caress and heal my spirit— from that day to this I have loved Jesus beyond the power of words to tell!" Martha must have felt something of this as she went to call her sister, "The Master is come, and calleth for thee."

Jesus had a greater blessing in store for them than the mere healing of a sickness that may or may not have been unto death. When Lazarus came forth from the tomb, their new-found joy was the sweeter against the dark background of their grief. He who has not experienced the joy of prayer that is answered after long delay, after much agonizing and heart-searching, after faith has been sorely tried, has missed one of the sweetest experiences of the Christian life. Oftentimes the answer is greater than the thing prayed for so long.

The other New Testament incident that seems to contradict the spirit of Jesus is the case of the Syrophoenician woman with the demon-possessed daughter. Jesus ignored her completely until the disciples said: "Send her away; for she crieth after us." It is not clear whether they meant to grant her request and get rid of her, or simply "get rid of her." Jesus answered: "I am not sent but unto the lost sheep of the house of Israel." This is the same Jesus that the disciples found talking to the woman of Samaria at Jacob's well, violating all the conventions regarding a rabbi talking alone with a woman, and regarding the traditional relationship between Jews and Samaritans. He turned to the woman, and said, "It is not meet to take the children's bread, and to cast it to dogs." Was that not enough to send the woman away in hurt and angry resentment, to fill her heart with discouragement and despair? But again, the woman's des-

perate need, her conviction that her cause was just, and
her faith in the power of Jesus, led her to persist,
humbly: "Truth, Lord: yet the dogs eat of the crumbs
which fall from their masters' table" (Matt. 15:27).
Jesus answered: "O woman, great is thy faith: be it unto
thee even as thou wilt." And her daughter was healed
"from that very hour."

An outstanding Old Testament instance of faithful
persistence is the night-long wrestling of Jacob with
God in the form of a man. Look for a moment at the
background of the story. God had already purposed to
bless Jacob as Abraham's successor as the patriarch of
the Chosen People. But Jacob took things in his own
hands. He cheated Esau out of his birthright and deceived his blind old father into giving him the blessing.
Then he fled to Haran, and there his uncle Laban
cheated him out of seven years' service. Jacob, in turn,
tricked Laban in a cattle deal and ran away at night
while his wives stole Laban's household gods. Jacob had
delayed over-long in obeying God's command: "Go
back to Bethel, and dwell there." Finally he heard that
Esau was coming to meet him, and fear overwhelmed
him. Following his familiar pattern, after he prayed that
God would deliver him, he sought to appease Esau's
imagined wrath with gifts.

If we read the passage closely, we see that *God was
wrestling with Jacob*. He was trying to get Jacob to confess his sins and acknowledge his need in complete surrender. Had Jacob received immediate assurance that
Esau's wrath would be appeased, he would have come
from that experience the same man he had been before,
relying upon trickery and sharp practices rather than
upon God. During that night of prayer, after Jacob had
been crippled for life, a new desire was born in his heart,

a desire for a greater blessing. That desire was granted. His name was changed from Jacob, which means "supplanter," to Israel, which means "prince with God." God won the victory, but it was also Jacob's victory. He called the name of the place Peniel: "For I have seen God face to face." Every person needs a Peniel as well as a Bethel.

Is it true that there is no need for importunity in prayer? Is it always true that when we ask, "quicker than the lightning's flash . . . the answer comes"? Not always. It was not so with Mary and Martha. It was not true in the case of the Syrophoenician woman. It was not so with Jacob at Peniel. It was not so with David. In Psalm 6:6 he cried: "I am weary with my groaning; all the night make I my bed to swim; I water my couch with my tears." But in verse 9 he affirmed: "The Lord hath heard my supplication; the Lord will receive my prayer."

"For we know not," Paul wrote, "what we should pray for as we ought: but the Spirit itself maketh intercession for us with groanings which cannot be uttered [with sighs too deep for words, RSV]." Why? To reach the ears, touch the heart, or change the mind of God? No. Men do not change the mind or purpose of God with their prayers. Some Old Testament evidence suggests that prayer has changed a *decree* of God in more than one instance. God told Moses in Exodus 32 that he intended to destroy Israel because of the golden calf they had made and worshiped. But Moses interceded for the people and recalled God's covenant with Abraham, Isaac, and Jacob: "And the Lord repented of the evil which he thought to do unto his people." After the purge, Moses pleaded again for the people, asking that they be forgiven: "And if not, blot me, I pray thee, out of thy book which thou hast written." Again, in 2 Kings 20:1–6 Isaiah declared God's message to King Hezekiah: "Set thine house in order; for thou shalt die, and not live." But bed-ridden Hezekiah prayed and "wept sore," and the Lord sent Isaiah back with this message: "I have heard thy prayer, I have seen thy tears . . . and I will add to thy days fifteen years." God's purpose took into account the heart and spirit of Moses, and also Hezekiah's strong faith, and his desire to see the city delivered from its enemies.

If prayer does not change the mind or purpose of God, some might ask, of what value is importunate prayer? Every argument used to deny the value or the necessity of importunate prayer may be used as logically to deny the value of any prayer. "Your Father knoweth what things ye have need of, before ye ask him" (Matt. 6:8). Then why ask? Why is it necessary for the Spirit to make intercession for us "with groanings which cannot be uttered"? Paul tells us that it is because we do not know what we should pray for, or how we ought to pray. *So the need for importunity lies with us and not with God.*

Perhaps we are coming to God with little piddling requests, when God is ready to give us something far greater than we ask. He may withhold the lesser blessing until our "wrestling in prayer" so strengthens our faith that we pray for the blessing God is ready to give.

Perhaps we need to be humbled with a sense of our utter dependence upon God more than we need what we are asking for. What we think is faith may be mere *self*-confidence. We may go serenely to God with the idea that surely he will give us what we ask, not because of his marvelous mercy and grace, but because of our own goodness and merit. We may pray like the Pharisee who thanked God that he was not like other men. Or we may go through the form of asking God for something, with the thought that if God doesn't give it us, we can get it for ourselves.

The place of persistent prayer may well become a place of self-realization, where we see ourselves in a new light. We who have gone to the place of prayer with supreme self-confidence may, by the necessity of importunity, come to discover hidden motives of selfishness, a lack of dependence upon God, unsuspected self-righteousness, or pride that has prevented a complete surrender of self-will. The *things* we have come to ask for sink into insignificance by the side of our greater need—the need for a closer walk with God. When we finally receive the desire of our heart, which we will receive if it is good for us, we find that we have been lifted to new heights of spiritual perception, and that the answer was greater than the asking.

Paul gives us still another reason for the Spirit's intercession: "He who searches the hearts of men knows what is the mind of the Spirit, because the Spirit intercedes for the saints *according to the will of God*" (Rom. 8:27, RSV). It is possible for us to pray for that which is *not* according to the will of God. Possibly the worst thing that could happen to us would be for God to grant us always what we pray for, that and nothing more.

God taught me that lesson some years ago. A situation had arisen in the church where I was pastor that made me unhappy. A brother pastor informed me that he had recommended me to another church. That seemed an unsought solution to my problem. I began to pray for *one thing:* that I should have an opportunity to appear before that church. The pulpit committee came to hear me, and invited me to visit the church. As I drove around through the community, I felt that my prayer had been answered. But when I stood up in the pulpit to preach, I seemed to stand alone and face a congregation of strangers. I was so familiar with the sermon that I had no difficulty in saying the words, but they seemed to be meaningless and to fall to the floor in front of me. I was out of contact with the Power from above, and out of contact with the congregation. Strangely enough, the pulpit committee was ready to recommend that the church call me. I was greatly embarrassed, but I had to tell them that the Lord was not in it, as far as I was concerned, and that if the church called I would have to decline.

Thereafter the burden of my prayers was that the Lord might have his perfect way in my ministry, as I served where he wanted me to serve. The church situation changed slowly, and eventually when a pulpit committee from another church invited me to supply their pulpit, I went reluctantly on a Wednesday night. When I stood in that pulpit I was at home, and I was not alone. Something as potent as an electric current united the congregation and me. They were my people, and I was their pastor. It was the beginning of a blessed pastorate of several years.

A well-known song urges: "take your burden to the Lord and leave it there." Someone has said that our trouble is that we take our burdens to the Lord, talk about them awhile, then pick them up and carry them away with us. We ought never to pray earnestly for anything unless we are willing to "pray it through," at whatever cost to ourselves. We must not forsake an earnest plea until God has shown us that what we are praying for is not best for us, or until we are at peace, knowing that in his good time the answer will come. Anything less leads to frustration and lack of faith. Anything less *is* lack of faith, either in God's power or in his beneficent purpose. If our prayer is selfish, God will show us wherein it is selfish. If what we want is not in line with his purpose for us, that also will be revealed, so that we will stop desiring it and accept the better thing, which is God's will for us. It is not always easy to say from the heart, "Thy will be done." We must never say it to excuse ourselves from "wrestling" until our hearts are at peace with God. But when we can say it joyously, we are on our way to victory.

Now the God of peace, that brought again from the dead our Lord Jesus, that great shepherd of the sheep, through the blood of the everlasting covenant, make you perfect in every good work to do his will, working in you that which is well-pleasing in his sight, through Jesus Christ; to whom be glory for ever and ever. Amen.